I HATE CAREGIVING

By

PAT COOK

PART - 1

I watched the painful expressions upon their faces. I watched tears well up in their eyes. I heard the pain of their grief in their voices. They grieved the gradual loss of their parent's memory. They grieved for their parents. They grieved for themselves. They grieved for the memories their parents have loss. Memories of them-their children. But not me.

I had just spent fourteen hours in a caregiver assistance education class. The class time was spread over four days. There were less than thirty people attending. Three men came the first day. Only one returned. Of all those attending, all were caring for parents. Of those attending, all were caring for victims of dementia related diseases, Alzheimer's or Parkinson's. But not me.

How were they-the caregiver children-going to apply the knowledge gained in this class-to the care of their parents? They were new to the process. Not me. I came to learn anything which would give me freedom. I didn't.

On the last day of class, a "Caregiver's Bill of Rights" was handed to each person. It was for them. It was not for me. I have no rights. I never did.

Caregiver right-1: I have the right to take care myself.

I have the right to take care myself. It will give me the capability of taking better care of my loved one. Yeah, right! I don't want to care for him. I have been caring for him since his release from the hospital, February, 2004. I am a prisoner. I am a slave. I hate it. I do not want to be a prisoner or a slave.

If people knew of my feelings, would they even care? If they did, would they condemn me for my feelings? Be repulsed by my hatred? Be turned away by my anger? "Be all you can be" is a mantra for many; for me it is a joke. I can be nothing more than a prisoner, a slave engulfed by my anger.

No one can see through the walls of this house. They cannot see the burden or the physical and psychic drain this burden has taken on me. I hate caring for a self-centered lazy man who refuses to talk or walk. I never thought one minute about not caring for my children. They were my children, my babies. I love them. They needed my love, attention, and care. This man is another issue. I think about caregiving for this man every minute of the day. I hate it.

He would never care for me as I have had to care for him. Once I strained my back and could not walk until the next day. He had to place me in the tub to soak and ease the muscles, per doctor's orders. He complained. He had to place me on the toilet. I had to have my spine on the rim, he complained because he had to adjust me.

If the caregiving burden was on him, I would be shipped out to a nursing home, so that he could have his freedom. But I cannot ship him out somewhere because there is no insurance or long-term care policy and no money. There is one limited life insurance policy amounting to about thirty thousand dollars. Just enough for burial expenses for him. He never planned on anything except what was in the next minute for himself. Not his family. For himself. His social security and state retirement together is twenty-one hundred dollars a month. Barely enough for all the bills.

An eighty-nine-year-old friend stops by almost every day. She brings flowers for him. But she comes to visit me. She was a caregiver to her husband for five years. Her husband could talk, but he could not get out of bed. Her husband was a big man. She is a small woman. She took care of him by herself until she could no longer bathe him. She got bathers from senior services to give him regular baths. She got a waterbed so that she could turn him or change linens easily. She said she almost threw him out of bed a few times when she bounced the bed to turn him over. Their funds were low because he had always been self-employed and she a housewife caring for many foster children. Her only biological son died in Vietnam. She draws a pension from her son, otherwise she would be penniless. She gets sixteen dollars in food stamps. Sixteen dollars for a whole month. With milk at $3.96, and bread at $2.39, $16.00 in food stamps does not go very far. If my husband died today, I would be in the same boat. Poverty stricken.

A social worker visited to assess the elderly couple's financial need. The social worker suggested a "divorce." The only way they could get any financial help was by getting a divorce and the state would pay her to care for him. The helpless bedridden man began to cry, "You wouldn't do that Mama, would you?" They did not get a divorce.

People rarely visited the couple during the five years she cared for him. She had no family to help her. Her only blood relative lives two hours away. She understands the isolation and the burden of caregiving. In response to her husband's death, she told me that she said, "Free at last. Thank God almighty, I am free at last." Although her words shocked me, they were true words of relief. Words I understood. She was no longer a prisoner or a slave to his needs.

Each day, this eighty-nine-year-old lady collects cast away flowers from Winn Dixie, and delivers them to shut-ins. Other days, she collects food from food banks and delivers to those in need. Always giving to others. Who is to care for her when she can no longer care for herself? Many have told her they understand the burden of caregiving. They do not. They have not been a caregiver. They are paying lip-service, nothing more. I do understand. I am the only one she knows who has this burden. She does not condemn me for my frustration, my anger, or my desire to have the burden gone. Anywhere out of my care so that I may have a life of my own.

The first time I left my husband at a Veteran's Respite facility, I felt like an escaped bird, free of its' cage. I was happy. For thirteen days, I was free to think and do things for myself, the first time in four years. When I began my trip back home, I began to cry. I cried the whole four-hour trip home. I did not want to return to slavery; to the prison of caregiving.

Caregiver right-2: I have the right to seek help from others.

I have the right to seek help from others. Yeah, right! When I first brought him home, I asked my mother to sit with him for a few hours. All she had to do was sit and watch TV. A simple task. She said, "No way." She never did. I had the right to ask her. December 1998, I was going to college full time and working two part-time jobs, but I still alternated nights with my brother-staying with her and Daddy; for three weeks before Daddy died.

I asked my oldest daughter to sit overnight in rehab. She couldn't take it. She stayed one night. I asked my middle daughter to spend one night. She never did. She has two children and a husband. A husband capable of caring for the children. She came to rehab with her husband and two children. I knew she did not come prepared to stay. So, I got up, walked out of rehab, and went home. She panicked. But she did not stay.

I did not ask my youngest daughter. I didn't have too. She took a leave of absence from her job. She got special permission for her son to go to a school near rehab. She stayed at rehab during the day, while I worked. I stayed at rehab during the night. We had too. My husband was on eighteen psychotropic drugs. He was out of his mind. But, doctors at Shand's Hospital in Gainesville, Florida and Tallahassee Memorial Hospital in Tallahassee, Florida refused to stop or reduce dosage. They assumed he was violent because he pulled out his tubes and lashed out against restraints. Restraints needed because he was on their drugs.

Caregiver right-3: I have the right to do things just for myself.

I have the right to do things just for myself. Yeah, right! I could write a book on that subject alone. I disappeared long ago. Maybe, I never developed. When did the robot take over? Emotionless robot. I am numb. I feel nothing but anger. I am empty, except for the anger.

January 1969, I married this man. I met him in October and married him in January. I did not know he was an only child. A spoiled only child. A hypochondriac. I should never have married him. But then I would not have had my two youngest daughters. But I could have gotten them from a sperm bank.

I had been married for five years to someone who married me because he thought my father had lots of money. Money my father would give to me. Boy, did he get fooled. My father gave me or us, no money. On our wedding day, my father over heard the guy's brother say, "You'll never have to worry about money now." I was naïve. Very naïve. As we drove pass the city limits, the jerk asked me, "Do you have money?" Our marriage was in time-frames of fifteen-month intervals; fifteen months together, fifteen months he was stationed with the Air Force in Goosebay, Labrador; and fifteen months of hell getting a divorce. I should have never re-married. But I had a daughter. I wanted a loving, happy perfect family for myself and my daughter. There is no such thing as a happy perfect family. The picture-perfect family doesn't exist. Only in dreams of the naïve. Or Norman Rockwell paintings of permanent smiles.

Caregiver right-4: I have the right to get angry, be depressed, and express feelings.

I have the right to get angry, be depressed, and express other difficult feelings occasionally. Yeah, right! I am angry. Very angry. I am depressed. Who wouldn't be depressed? I am trapped. I am resentful. I only feel a tiny bit of guilt for this. But I have legitimate cause and he knows it. I told him before, but he never listened. Now he can't escape to a friend's house or say "I am not your enemy". He has always been the enemy. He was and is self-absorbed. Family neglected.

Caregiver right-5: I have the right to reject any attempt to manipulate me.

I have the right to reject any attempt to manipulate me. Yeah, right! I have tried to escape the manipulation- all the years of our married life. But I have lived under the oppression of my father and husband. No worth for the female. Females have no brains. Females have no penis and balls. Therefore, their ideas and opinions do not have worth.

My mother acknowledged my worthlessness. I was forced to take over my mother's business when she retired. I did not want too. My husband, my father, and my mother insisted it was a gold mine. AH! It may have been a gold mine for them but it was a big fat money pit. It was a gold mine for my mother. Buy, I only got the shaft.

I had helped my mother on the days she prepared monthly reports. She paid me three dollars an hour. But as soon as I took over, she said, "You need to hire my brother and pay him five dollars an hour."

"Mother, you only paid me three dollars an hour." I responded.

"Yeah. But he has a family to support."

My thought was, "Why the hell didn't she force him to take over instead of forcing me." Needless to say. I never hired him or anyone. The business didn't support one person. Worthless. Confirmation. I was worthless, or at the very least worth only three dollars an hour.

Caregiver right-6: I have the right to receive consideration, affection, forgiveness, and acceptance for what I do.

I have the right to receive consideration, affection, forgiveness, and acceptance for what I do. Yeah, right! I have never received that. Never will.

Caregiver right -7: I have the right to take pride in what I am accomplishing and applaud the courage it has sometimes taken to meet the needs of my loved one.

I have the right to take pride in what I am accomplishing and applaud the courage it has sometimes taken to meet the needs of my loved one. Yeah, right! I am an unpaid slave. A servant. The position I did not know I was being forced into upon marrying this man forty plus years ago. Not just recently. He liked to say he was not my enemy. Yeah, right! He was the enemy. He had me trapped then, paralyzed then, and trapped more, paralyzed more, now. I should have left years ago. I have legitimate cause and he knows it. I should have taken my children. Left him alone. An adult only child. Orphaned only child. We are his only family. No relatives here. No relatives there. Orphaned. My parents loved him more than me. And he, he loved my father so much he asked my mother if he could be buried at my father's feet.

Caregiver right-8: I have the right to protect my individuality and right to make a life for myself without taking care of him/her.

I have the right to protect my individuality and right to make a life for myself without taking care of him. Yeah, right! I will probably die before he does.

I don't know who made up the Caregiver Bill of Rights, but one thing I do know is that these rights are a big pile of crap. They were probably written by some big shot psychologist who has never been a caregiver.

No one wants anyone to know their true feelings about caregiving. People smile and say, "I don't know how you do it." You the caregiving just smile; wanting to scream behind the smile, "I hate caregiving."

Someone needs to say it, and so I choose to say it here, "I HATE CAREGIVING."

Part - 2

PREVENTIVE MEDICINE

Preventative medicine. What a joke! The county had enlisted Capital Health Plan as their insurance provider. CHP practices preventative medicine. CHP pays one hundred percent of hospital cost. Blue Cross/Blue Shield pays eighty percent. Twenty percent of anything would bankrupt us. Just before the county changed to Blue Cross/Blue Shield, CHP found a miniscule brain aneurism. Pow! My hypochondriac husband had something new to fixate on. He became fixated on curing the aneurism. He did not need surgery. It was elective.

In 2003, I became employed with a small company in Tallahassee, Florida. They used CHP as their insurance provider. My husband was excited. He could now discuss the brain aneurism with doctors. He was told, "If the aneurism burst you will have a headache like you have never had before".

Two procedures were available for an aneurism. A coil inserted to fill up the aneurism bubble or open the head and clip the aneurism. No doctors in Tallahassee used coils to fill an aneurism, they only opened the head. The nearest doctor was in Gainesville, Florida. The Shand's Hospital Doctor's name was Mericle (Miracle). Unfortunately, he did not perform miracles.

Dr. Mericle performed the coil procedure, but the aneurism opening was too large and it was not filled with the coil. Dr. Mericle talked my hypochondriac husband into doing what he did not want. He did not want to open his head.

My husband tried to justify opening his head by declaring he did not want to have an accident caused by the rupture of the aneurism, resulting in someone getting hurt. My husband tried to get everyone around him to make the decision for him. I was anxious about the surgery. He tried to get me to make the decision to operate. I told him it was not my head and not my decision. I FORGOT HE WAS A HYPOCHONDRIAC. I forgot because I normally ignored his feigned illnesses.

Unfortunately for my husband, for me and our family, a medical mistake happened. Dr, Mericle performed life altering surgery without providing a clear understanding that it could possibly alter speech function. Altering speech functions of a motor-mouth individual scatters life style. At no time did they ever say: This surgery may cause a stroke. This surgery may cause a loss of speech. No, never. Had this motor-mouth ever had been told he could lose his speech he would never have had the surgery. He loved to talk more than breathe. Dr. Mericle said my husband would be in the hospital four days. That did not change when he opened the head. Four months in the hospital and rehab later, he came home.

CHP provided a wheelchair and a Hemi-walker. But never a brace for his ankle. CHP's follow-up medical care was limited. They divert people with problematic or continuing medical issues away from the normal population of patients. Unfortunately, the doctor to whom all were referred was uncomfortable with his new patients. He didn't say so. But his every action spoke loudly to me. I do not remember his name, but I shall never forget his behaviors. Every appointment, I pushed my stroke victim husband's wheelchair into his office. My husband's right arm paralyzed; he could walk with a Hemi walker, but his right ankle was weak. Most of all, my motor-mouth husband could not talk. The doctor **NEVER LOOKED EITHER OF US IN THE EYE**. He always looked away from us. He answered limited questions always with his eyes to our right or left, never straight forward and he shifted uneasily in his chair. He made me nervous.

CHP is supposed to be the best of medical care. But their follow-up was greatly lacking.

=2=

AFTERMATH OF SURGERY

My husband did exactly as he has always done. He followed his own rules. He smoked before his surgery. He got the coil procedure to fill the brain aneurism. It didn't work. He got his head opened when he had gone to Shand's Hospital to prevent opening his head. All of us were apprehensive, but we did not make the decision to open his head. He did. He said, "he didn't want to be a guinea pig at Shand's because it is a teaching hospital". Dr. Mericle assured him he would do the surgery not a student. Shand's Hospital at the University of Florida in Gainesville, Florida has traditionally been a hospital of hope for many. But for me, my children, and my husband, Shand's ruined our lives

November 6, 2003 changed our lives forever. Dr. Mericle said, "The surgery went fine". They always do.   If the patient doesn't die on the table, everything went fine. Dr. Mericle said, "I always check the clamps before I close the head. Some doctors don't. But I do. When I tested the clamp, it did not hold, I retested the clamp and it held. Then I closed his head. He is doing fine." Dr. Mericle did not tell us what to expect after surgery. He should have.

We were allowed to take turns going into intensive care. What does the medical profession keep a secret, especially about brain surgery? Television programs show neatly wrapped heads, tubes hanging out of mouth or nose, and blinking machines. We were in a state of shock when confronted with the image which lay on the bed.

In the movie "Total Recall", Arnold Schwarzenegger's nemesis is a big guy with a head as big and round as a beach ball. That is exactly what my husband looked like. Except my husband had tubes from everywhere. That is what met us in the intensive care recovery room. On the other hand, my brother was hit by a car and had massive head injury; his head did not swell like my husband's.

Our two young grandchildren were allowed in see him. Although they were warned of the difference in his appearance, they wanted to see him anyway. I believe it unfair of the medical profession to keep such obvious physical changes to themselves. The families need this information to prepare for the shock.

On November 7, 2003 a CT scan showed my husband had a middle cerebral artery stoke. In other words, at the area of the aneurism clipping. What happened? One: the brain was exposed longer than in normal head openings and two: a serious medication error in intensive care. Dr. Mericle confirmed the brain was exposed longer than normal. Medical records show they allowed my husband to wake after head closed; although groggy he was able to move both right and left at command.

But for the medical "incident", a young male intensive care nurse explained a medication error to my youngest daughter. One medication must slowly level out as the substitute medication is slowly added. At equal levels the original is removed. It did not happen in that order. It was just "an incident." As the young intensive care nurse is explaining the error, the total intensive care went silent. A deep hush. A revelation of things to be kept quiet. Intensive care nurses focused their attention to the young nurse. Strong disapproving stares were directed to toward him. The quieter the room got and the stares directed to the young nurse-the more uneasy he became. He realized he did something wrong. He told the truth. My youngest daughter is very observant and notices body language more than any person I know. She was fully aware of the sounds, body language, and stares of the intensive care room. She said, "You could hear a pin drop."

When my husband began waking, he began questioning an intensive care doctor who was at bedside. With tubes down his throat, he could not get the doctor's attention. The doctor was ignoring him and talking to my youngest daughter. My husband reached out grabbed the doctor's jacket. The doctor went out, ordered my husband sedated and his left wrist tied down. They assumed he was violent and more drugs added.

When sluggishly-he protested the binding of his hand, he fought angrily against the restraints, getting his left arm free he pulled tubes out. They added more psychotropic drugs. Declaring he was violent. We protested the tied downs and the drugs. They never listened.

My husband never cuffed prisoners when he transported them for the sheriff's office. Now he and we found him bound and drugged.

From the doctors and nurses, my youngest daughter was able to extract information about her father. But me, when I asked a question, I was diverted to ask someone else. Someone not present or someone not available. Doctor Mericle was a vanishing act and unreachable after the surgery. Before surgery-he was easy to reach and talk too. Other doctors were not forthcoming with answers to questions or a request to transfer my husband to a Tallahassee hospital nearer our home. I was ignored. Mostly, my husband slept when I was present at the hospital.

I do not remember anyone telling us he had had a stroke for several days after the surgery. When they did, they said it was "a mild stroke" and passed it off as a normal occurrence in this type of operation. Weeks later, I was trying to get him transferred to the Tallahassee hospital, the young student doctor said, "He had a massive stroke." That is when my middle daughter looked at me in surprise declaring, "You told me it was mild stroke!" And so, it went. Misinformation every day. This same young doctor needed a lot more training in bedside manners. Her final comments to us: She screamed, "He will die if you transfer him to Tallahassee!" And so, it went. If he was transferred, he would die and if he stayed, he would die because they wanted to do more surgeries, more training for the student doctors.

My husband had been using a CPAP machine for sleep apnea for several years. Shand's nurses tried many times to place the CPAP mask upon his face during hospital stay. But he fought or pulled it off. Eight days after surgery, still in intensive care drugged, and still on ventilatory tubes. The doctors were insistent that the tubes needed to be removed. I was approached to allow a tracheotomy on November 14, 2003. Although this was beyond approval of the first surgery, I did allow it. The trach was a good thing because it is a radical solution for sleep apnea. He has not used a CPAP machine since the tracheotomy and his snoring had stopped.

After the trach he contacted pneumonia. On November 16, 2003, his red blood cell count dropped to 18.2, he was started on a Protonix drip and blood transfusions. He was given multiple blood transfusions over several days to bring the red blood count just above 30. Stabilized for several more days without transfusions he was transferred to an intermediate floor for several weeks. He was transferred to a regular floor where he stayed until December 12, 2003. He developed right lower extremity pain. A Doppler which shown to be Deep Vein thrombus, he was started on heparin. Returned back to intermediate floor because a CT showed a pulmonary embolus. He was monitored for several days.

I began asking for a transfer to Tallahassee Memorial Hospital, Shand's doctors repeatedly demanded to place a feeding tube into my husband's stomach. Even though they had not tried any soft foods. I may not be the smartest cookie in the box, but even I know that a man fighting against restraints, drugged, pulling out tubes and trach is going to pull a feeding tube from his belly. Several doctors told me, "He will starve to death if we don't put in the feeding tube." My response to that was, "It wouldn't hurt him to lose a few pounds." And so, it went. All doctors began a continual request to remove the feeding tube from nose and to put a feeding tube in his stomach. I held steadfast against Shand's doing any other surgeries. I was not stupid. If he is out of his mind, pulling tubes from his arms, his nose, and getting free of restraints what a crazy idea to put a tube in his stomach.

Putting in a stomach feeding tube would therein create another problem from peritonitis, possible internal bleeding and possible death. Apparently, they needed class practice on inserting stomach tubes. My husband had lost a lot of weight since November 6th. That was a good thing. Yet, I was reprimanded about letting him starve to death. He did not want to be a practice case. I would not let them operate further.

About December 15, 2003, the transfer to TMH happened. Immediately upon arrival at TMH the doctors began the same chorus of feeding tube. I held my ground. They had him eating ice cream. His trach was permanently removed. Two days in TMH, I was told he did not need to be to be there. He was shipped across the street to TMH rehab. There again I was bombarded with demands for feeding tube, this time by the social worker. I recounted with, "You bring a gastrointestinal doctor to discuss it and I will decide then." As usual, doctor's visits are when I am not at bedside.

The social worker met me at bedside to say the Gastro doctor had visited with my husband. She reported, "The doctor said that with your husband pulling out his trach and tubes it would not be wise to put in a stomach tube." When she reported the doctor's statements which confirmed my stand against a feeding tube. She seemed disappointed when I said, "Exactly! That is exactly why I was not going to let a surgery happen. He would have pulled the tube out and created greater problems." That was the end of discussion of stomach feeding tube. But they did not reduce meds. He did not die from the move to Tallahassee. Nor did he die from not putting in a stomach tube.

Again, I protested the psychotropic drugs given at Shand's and continued at TMH rehab. All too deaf ears. My husband was out of his mind. TMH rehab did not tie him down and he refused to keep the sheets over his half naked body, even when family and a few friends stopped by. He wore only a T-shirt. We positioned the curtains so that no one could see his genitals. Three visitors, other than family members, came by to see him in rehab. He still would not keep the sheet on.

My youngest daughter took a three-month medical leave from her job to stay with her father at TMH Rehab during the day. She got specially permission for her son to go to a school nearby while I continued to work in four counties. She did this because the rehab wouldn't guarantee his safety 24/7. She didn't have to be asked. She just jumped in to help.

When she arrived, my husband was in a partial drug induced coma with the eighteen psychotropic drugs. When the drugs wore off and he became somewhat lucid, he threw off his covers and tried to get out of bed.

Our middle daughter is quick tempered and rarely controls her temper or her tongue. She was visiting and I had stepped out. She overheard two TMH Rehab nursing aides, in the hallway, commenting loudly about the patients. One made a comment, "You should see the one down the hall, he lays around naked." Followed by laughter. Our daughter realized the aide was talking about her father, she jumped up, ran into the hallway. "You do not have to come in here and see him either." The aides hurried down the hallway.

TMH Rehab let my drugged husband fall out of the bed. I had to insist he be x-rayed. The ambulance drivers appeared to be annoyed that they had to transport him across the street to the hospital. They delivered him to the hospital, but not before slamming his paralyzed arm into the brackets which hold the gurney in place within the ambulance. In the hospital, the ambulance drivers parked the gurney in the hospital hallway just outside the x-ray department doorway. They shouted to the x-ray department's open doorway. They did not check to see if anyone was actually in the x-ray room, before they marched off down the hall.

The gurney was positioned with my husband's left arm to the wall. I was standing next to the gurney on his right side, waiting for someone to appear from the open doorway. My husband, being under the influence of the psychotropic drugs, removed his good left arm from the gurney straps. He began pushing himself away from the left wall. He was fighting the straps-trying to get up. I braced myself against the gurney and shouted for help. It was several minutes before anyone appeared. Had I not been with him, I would have had a law suit against the ambulance drivers and the hospital.

But, then again it could have been like the cover-up for incompetence at Shand's Hospital which attributed to his stroke. No record can be found of the incident. That was very convenient.

When I began getting his records, I was asked by records clerk, "Do you think the records were altered?" I responded, "Yes. There is no record anywhere of the described incident. Months later, I was talking with a retired nurse who confirmed "records are altered at hospitals" with a "threat of being fired it they did not alter the records". Her statements to me brought back the events in the movie "THE VERDICT" with Paul Newman. The movie exposed altering hospital records.

I was trying to continue working during the day, while our youngest daughter stayed at rehab. On her first day at rehab, she attended physical therapy with her father, he was asleep (drugged). What point is physical therapy good for a drugged man? Following the session, she had a discussion with the therapist. The therapist said, she "couldn't do anything with him because they had him drugged so much".

Our daughter requested a meeting with the Rehab head nurse. The head nurse refused to take him off the drugs. Then, she requested a meeting with the director of the rehab; that meeting with the director, the head nurse, and two CHP representatives. The director tried to justify my husband being drugged by saying, "He needs to be on these medications because he becomes aggressive when he comes off the drugs." Her response to the director and everyone else was, "There is a big difference between aggression and confusion. Dad is confused, you have him drugged up and he doesn't know where he is or what is going on…that is not aggression".

Med's dosage was reduced minimally. He became more alert and aware of his situation and what had happened to him. He started physical therapy and started to get stronger. At the last rehab physical therapy session, the therapist said, "I am glad you came because your dad would not be where he is today if you wouldn't have…he now has a chance to live".

=3=

FOUR MONTHS AFTER SURGERY

He was only supposed to be in the hospital for three or four days. November 6, 2003 till February 18, 2004. Four months he stayed. He could not talk to the visitors or us. Because of the fourteen psychotropic drugs, we were not truly aware of my husband's condition. Not until I brought him home and weaned him off the drugs.

February 18, 2004, my husband was loaded into my car and I took him home. Although still drugged, he was able to assist getting in the car. He could not walk, his right arm paralyzed, and he was unable to talk. I blindly filled all the drug prescriptions we were given upon his release.

That night, I gave him the prescribed dosage of glyburide. He had an insulin shock seizure and 911 was called. The ambulance couldn't find our house, which is less than a mile from the hospital and on a major street. They said they were recruited to drive the ambulance because the hospital was shorthanded.

They carried him out on a gurney and put into the ambulance. I locked up the house and got in my car. The ambulance was sitting unmoved. I looked in the back and they were doing things I thought should be done at the hospital. They said his blood pressure was going up. I thought the only thing going up was the hospital bill. The ER doctor said, "He has lost over one hundred pounds. He doesn't need glyburide." One medicine deleted.

On February 28, 2004, he had a convulsion. I panicked, called 911. Then I handed the phone to my upset nine-year-old grandson and told him to call his aunt for help. My husband was flown to Tallahassee Memorial Hospital ER. He was treated and released.

He did not return to any hospital until June 2011. He had an umbilical cord hernia. The doctor pushed it back in place.

=4=

STROKE, APHASIA AND APRAXIA

Stroke is a family crisis where every member of the family unit is impacted. The effects of stroke dictate the amount of adjustment the individual, the family unit and the family caregiver must undertake to adapt to the new experience. Their individual resilience and coping strategies make successful outcomes of post-stroke quality of life.

"Previous stroke research has indicated that depression is the biggest psychiatric problem following stroke and if a stroke survivor has depression, it is most likely the family caregiver does also. Depression is difficult to identify in stroke induced aphasia victims. However there remains an important gap in the current literature regarding whether aphasia is curable and whether in home rehabilitation and therapy works (Cook, 2009)."

Aphasia and apraxia, I had never heard the words. Stroke. I have heard of stroke and the impact it has on the human organism which we inhabit. Yet, I have never experienced stroke or aphasia or apraxia in my family. My husband had elective brain surgery which gave him both.

Aphasia and apraxia are similar. Aphasia is a speech-language disorder which produces many forms of speech disruption as a direct result of brain injury location (Broca's aphasia. Retrieved 7/12/2011 from neurology.health-cares.net/Brocas-aphasia.php). Apraxia victims have trouble saying what they want to say correctly with consistency without interruption of comprehension (Apraxia. Retrieved 7/12/2011, from www.nidcd.nih.gov/directory).

Aphasia and apraxia for a "motor-mouth" talkative, outgoing individual is a life altering event. The family roles no longer exist for him. He is the stroke victim. He is language impaired aphasic and apraxia stroke victim. We the family unit face physical, cognitive and personal adjustment challenges to adapt to his loss of speech, loss of mobility, depression and disruption of quality of life. We know-we are there.

The middle cerebral artery stroke is the result of a brain infarction. This focal neurologic deficit produces diverse neurological complications. My husband's surgery was on the left side of his brain. The left side of the brain is supplied by the middle cerebral artery's superior division which is the location of Broca's area of language expression and the location of Wernicke's area of language comprehension. Damage to the dominant hemisphere of the brain, which is primarily the left hemisphere, results in either Broca's or Wernicke' aphasia.

Damage to Wernicke's area produces fluent aphasia which means they have difficulty speaking in coherent sentences, without comprehension of their errors of speech. Damage to Broca's area produces non-fluent aphasia which means they have comprehension but have difficulty expressing themselves. Global aphasia produces difficulty understanding language and limited ability to speak. Other types of aphasia have difficulty naming objects or understanding their uses (Aphasia. Retrieved July 7, 2011 from MedicineNet, Inc.).

My husband's stroke produced Broca's aphasia, apraxia and right arm paralysis with curled fingers, and a weak right ankle. Comprehension is not problem for him. He must learn to connect the words to his mouth. Expression in single words is difficult, yet repetitive sentences produce only minimal difficulty. But he does not want to work at relearning to over-come the aphasia or apraxia. He had rather play Charades or write notes. Writing notes is easy for him but spelling is not. He "tries" to draw pictures to describe what he wants to say…yet refuses to try to speak.

=5=

HOME PREPARATIONS

My father died Christmas day 1998. Mother gave me his hospital bed for my husband. Before removing my husband from the hospital, I purchased a new mattress for the bed. I just could not see my husband lay on the mattress where my father had died. It was just me.

During the first two months after returning home, my youngest daughter and I developed our own personal therapy and stress relief. A large shed was attached to my carport and we both took turns reducing that shed to rubble. With each swing of the sledgehammer, we beat out our frustration at doctors and such. We took it all out on the shed. She returned to work in Ocala and on the weekends, she swung that sledgehammer. We swung and swung until the shed was gone. But our frustration still remained.

For the first two months after returning home, our youngest and I had to help my husband get in and out of the bed and push him around the house in his wheelchair. We prepared his meals, but he was able to feed himself using his left hand. Reducing his medications increased our awareness of the extent of the stroke. Decreased right arm movement. Curved fingers. We could verify the decreased amount of right leg, knee, and ankle movement. We could hear the difficulty of speech formation. Finally, all psychotropic drugs removed from his system. He was back to his old self except for the inconvenient effects of the stroke. His comprehension was still intact and he read the newspaper every day.

We explored and tried to put in handicap grab bars next to the toilet. That did not work because placement was not proper for pulling and sitting or pulling and standing up. The laundry room door prevented proper placement. He decided to use the laundry room door handle as his grab bar. He was able to pull himself up from the wheelchair and sit on toilet. That did work successfully.

I taught him how to loop his right curved thumb and fingers in the waist band of his shorts, so that he could pullup his shorts after using the toilet. A therapist taught him how to put on his own shirts. A therapist showed him how to help himself by exercising his arm and hand. A therapist taught him how to move his body forward in the wheelchair to gain balance and transfer to bed or toilet. He complied with their orders in their presence. But not before, I was completely exhausted from pulling and tugging on him.

About year two, I let him put his pills in a pill minder. A form of independence regained. Once he began splitting some pills. I took the bottle because I did not remember the pills requiring splitting. The label did not say to split. I instructed him to always read the labels.

He likes pills. He is a hypochondriac. In 2009, we were temporarily renting a house in Naples, Florida, he had some complaint which I addressed with Tylenol. Apparently, he was angry I did not give him more. I had Tylenol extra strength and Tylenol PM in the same kitchen drawer. Later when I opened the drawer-all Tylenol bottles were gone. I did not say a word. About eleven pm, he calls me to feel his pacemaker. The pacemaker, which operates on demand, was racing. I asked if he wanted to go to the hospital. No-he did not. I finally realized he had taken all the remaining Tylenol PM which slowed his heart rate.

I called VA about checking the pacemaker. They had no way to do so. I tried to locate the manufacture-to no avail. Okay we will address it at a VA appointment. I let them give him an EKG, without disclosing the pills. On the follow-up visit a week later, I told the primary doctor what he had taken to activate the pacemaker. He didn't deny it. The doctor ignored the issue.

=6=

BATHING

Bathing was a challenge. We do not have a walk-in shower. We have a tub. I purchased a large tub bench. The bath bench will not fit completely in the tub. Two legs out. Two legs in tub. He backs up to the bath bench. Bracing himself with his left arm on the sink. He lowers himself on the extended end of the bench, turns toward his right side to slide further on the bench. I used to put his right leg in the tub, but as he has gotten stronger, he now lends back allowing his body to pull the right leg almost over the rim. I have to finish putting his foot into the tub. He is facing the water handles, his right side to the bath wall.

While he sat on the toilet, I had undressed him. He transferred to the wheelchair and moved next to tub. So went the bath procedures. But nothing in life is easy.

All bathing routines followed same steps. Until a few months after his return home, he was moving his legs, left on top of right to push leg under tub bench. He slipped. In slow motion, he went down. Slippery and wet, I could not hold him. So, I quickly placed my hand over the water spout to prevent injury. He was fully a tangled lump under the tub bench. I pulled his legs untangled and called 911.

The ambulance arrived-one tall guy and one short. They called for reinforcement. Two firefighters arrived to help. The four guys pulled him free of the tub. Placed his naked wet body on a gurney and wheeled him to his room. He thanked them. I thanked them. Off they went.

Bathing my husband is a chore. As he gets larger it is an exhausting chore. A chore I do not want to do. In year one post stroke, I washed him everywhere but genital. Then I thought, "Why am I doing this? There is nothing wrong with his left hand and arm. I introduced a new routine. I wet his hair and body. I pour shampoo on his head. He washes his hair. I must have two washcloths nearby because he fusses if he gets water or shampoo in or near his eyes. Therefore, one is to wipe away shampoo or water. Without rinsing hair, I massage body wash into the other washcloth and wash his back, his left arm and left hand. I then give him the washcloth to wash his belly, right arm, right hand, face and ears. Then, I rinse his upper body and head.

He drives me nuts! Apparently, he has never used a washcloth to bathe, assuming he would be clean by soaping all over and rubbing with his hand was sufficient cleansing. After I rinse his upper body, he insists on the water continuously running over his body as he rubs himself all over, scrubbing with his hand-not washcloth-in the areas already scrubbed with a washcloth. Annoying it is.

The lower body bath begins by adding more body wash to washcloth. I wash the left thigh and left leg and foot, then push the soapy washcloth under the left side of his fat belly roll and scrub as best as possible with the belly in the way. Then I move bath attention to right leg and foot reaching far over the tub, pushing the washcloth under the right-side belly fat and scrub. I put the washcloth in his left hand, he washes his genitals as he moans and groans pulling and washing the penis skin and balls.

To get out of the tub requires him to move his left leg over the tub rim and turn his body to get out. He cannot lift his right leg over the rim. His body turns with left leg out of tub, he moves his right knee to tub rim. There he sits with right leg in tub. I must pull the right leg up over the rim. Early post-stroke, the right leg did not feel like it weighs fifty pounds. Now it does.

His bottom does not get a good scrub because he won't stand up in the tub. The children think he is smelly because he doesn't get his butt washed with a washcloth. I put a small towel on the bath bench to allow water to get under his bottom. He sometimes stinks because he does not clean himself very well after using the toilet. He uses toilet paper, then disposable wipes, but does not do a very good job sometimes. He no longer wears underwear, so I place a small towel on the seat of the wheelchair so he won't get poop smears on the chair seat. He wears only a T-shirt to bed; this is to allow him to use a urinal during the night.

I allowed my youngest daughter to care for him for six months. I told her if she moved into a house which would accommodate him and his wheelchair-I would let her take him. Give me a break and also get him into therapy, again. I felt free those six months-although she wouldn't admit it-it was a burden for her. She insisted she had bath service for him, similar to what we have with senior services in north Florida. The bath service was her housemate and herself. I didn't think her giving him a bath was appropriate. But she started doing it without my knowledge. She had moved into a larger house. It had a step-in shower with sliding doors. She removed the doors and they got him in for shower. Showers more often that I had been doing. He stood for the showers and she and her male housemate gave him a scrub-even his bottom. She let him wash himself except those areas he couldn't reach.

July 2009, we moved to Naples, Florida so that I could look for work within a fifteen-minute drive from the house. Searching for the perfect house, I took a measuring tape, measured doorways and examined bathrooms in many houses. Only one met our needs of large doorways and walk-in shower. He didn't like the shower. One bath is all he allowed. No more. He refused to bathe in the shower. It was too small for him. He was uneasy with stepping into it and getting out of it. Our grandson was visiting and I asked him to help me get the man out of the shower. So now what? He can't. No. He will not get in the shower.

"Well, then you are going to bathe in the yard." I spoke. I purchased a Y-shaped hose, a garden hose, and a spray nozzle from Home Depot. I prepared an outside bath area by stringing a clothes line just outside a side door. I attached one end of the line to an iron pipe attached to the house. I wrapped the line twice around a palm tree and attached the other end to a cluster of palms. Over the clothes line, I draped two large sheets-one on the west side and one on the south side to provide privacy on two sides, the house bordered the north side, and the fourth side provided a good tail wind. I am kidding. To the south a border of trees and shrubs ten feet deep provides cover from an office building. To the west tall shrubs block a view of the street. To the east is a border of under brush and trees forty-feet deep. I just hoped no one had binoculars in the three tall buildings across the six-lane highway.

The side door is next to the laundry room window and close to the new outside bath area. I removed the window screen and placed it between the inside wall and dryer. I turned off the hot and cold spigots to the washing machine and removed the hoses. I attached the Y-hose and the spray nozzle to the garden hose. I attached the Y-hose to the hot and cold spigots and turned on the spigots to test for leaks. No leaks. I test water temperature. I call "his majesty" to come check the water temperature. When the water is adjusted to his satisfaction, I open the window of the laundry room and stick the garden hose with spray nozzle attached, out the window. Shower ready.

Okay, I am almost ready to give him a bath. I am already tired, ignore myself and continue. I instruct him to get in his electric powerchair and go around to the side of the house for his bath. He transfers to the chair as I move his hemi-walker and a small towel outside to the prepared bath area. In the bath area, I have placed his bath bench and covered the top with a small towel. Just inside the side door I have placed body wash, shampoo, two washcloths and two towels.

I meet him at the front door and open it. He drives the powerchair out the door, rolls down the sidewalk which runs around the house to the side door. I close the front door; walk through the kitchen, through the laundry, through the den and out the back door just in time to meet "his majesty" for his bath. I pull back the sheet on the west side. I give him the hemi-walker and he stands up. I move the powerchair ten-feet away from area as he turns around to back up to the bench. Twice he has dropped his shorts before I have closed the sheet. I just hope no one was passing by on the street. They would have seen the flasher. When he sits on the bench, I remove his shorts from his ankles. He removes his T-shirt and glasses and hands them to me. I pull the garden hose through the laundry room window and mash the spray nozzle to let out some water until the temperature is reached for bathing. I spray him all over and begin the bath. The difference in location allows variation to the bath ritual; I can move around the body. But the same procedure is followed as in a normal bathroom.

The bath complete, I give him the hemi-walker and he stands. I dry his head and body, instruct him to turn around, and drape the towel down his back. I move the powerchair close to the back of his legs and move the sheet aside, he sits down. With second towel, I dry his legs and feet and set them on the foot rest of the chair. I place the towel I used to dry his legs and

feet, over his lap. I wipe off his glasses and give them to him and off he goes to the front door. I

meet him at the front door and step outside to watch the front wheels of his chair. If he does not

approach the door opening at the correct speed or wheel position the chair will pitch him

forward. Or he gets stuck with the small wheels inside and the back large wheels spinning

rubber. Once inside, he must be dressed; deodorant under left arm-give deodorant to him. I lift

his right arm, which is very heavy, and hold it up until he finishes applying deodorant. I help

him put on T-shirt, his feet in his shorts and give him the hemi-walker. He loops his right fingers

into the top of the shorts, like I taught him to do, and we pull up his shorts as he stands. His job

is to get into his regular wheelchair and put on his shoes. My job is to undo all the bath

preparation and put towels and bed linens in washing machine-after I take a break.

=7=

TOILET

He tried to get me to wipe his butt. No way, it belongs to him. I wiped my children's butts

because they did not know how. He is not my child. He knows how. He had to adjust to using

his left hand.

People and animals deposit poop in different shapes. Cow poop plop forms large moon

shaped flat piles (cow patties). Rabbits poop small balls into clutters as do a lot of small critters.

Horses poop is the size of fists. My husband usually poops like a horse. Even before his stroke

he stopped up the toilet-all the time. Horse sized poop with toilet paper and disposable wipes,

clog toilets. I do a lot of things with tools, carpentry, sawing, painting, floor tiles, and repairs everywhere. I do not do electrical and plumbing repairs. I do not like plunging a toilet-under any conditions. But I have too.

Peeing and pooping are an unpleasant chore. I had to get a plastic raised toilet seat because our original toilet was too low and forced him to squat with difficulty. He was always very apprehensive sitting down on the raised plastic toilet seat. Afraid it would slip-so be I. Once he was seated, I could walk away. I have seen plastic raised toilet seats which appeared firmly attached, this one was not. It was smelly and no amount of bleach would cure the scent. Sometimes bowl excrement would back wash into the raised seat. I hated that thing. Months of the watching him sitting on it and my cleaning it-drove me nuts.

I decided there had to be a better way. I measured the toilet-floor to top rim of plastic seat. Eighteen inches. I went to Lowe's and Home Depot to find a toilet which reaches eighteen inches. I successfully found a seventeen-inch-high toilet-which in place with a normal toilet seat attached is perfect. No more stinky plastic raised toilet seat-into the trash it went.

I have now bought three seventeen-inch toilets-one for our house-one for my youngest daughter's rental house and one for the house I rented in Naples, Florida. Although, we didn't ask permission to replace the toilets in rental property-the landlord's profited from the switch. As a landlord, I would appreciate any improvement made to my houses at the renter's expense.

I have to escort him to restrooms in public spaces, he cannot go alone. He can go alone in our home because I have a high toilet and left grab bar. I must take him into the ladies' restrooms because men restrooms contain urinals and exposure of men peeing.

While traveling in Palm Beach, Florida, I wanted to tour a mansion of some famous person, something to do with trains. I was pushing my husband around and he saw the public restroom.

Here we go again. He never wants to wait. Always the inspector. I always check the lady's restroom to see if anyone is in there. When all clear, I take him in. I was getting him into the stall-when a snooty lady walked in. She looked at me strangely, opened the door to see if she had read the sign wrong. I just told her to come on in and go to the last stall.

=8=

SPEECH LESSONS

CHP is supposed to be the best medical care. But their follow-up was greatly lacking. A month after returning home, in hopes of returning my now non-verbal husband to a somewhat normal speech pattern, CHP scheduled a speech therapist for weekly appointments at the TMH rehab. I took him to speech therapy. The therapist told us she "only worked with children and not accustom to teaching adults". She was uncomfortable with my husband. She was confused how to proceed. On our second visit, our nine-year old grandson accompanied us. We realized she was still ineffective. Our grandson realized she was ineffective and he TOOK OVER speech training. He was nine. My grandson accomplished what she did not. He got him to say the words. It was as if a light bulb appeared over the therapist head.

After CHP's comedy of sending a children's speech therapist to teach a sixty-two-year-old stroke victim, I found new resources. I enrolled him in the speech therapy clinic at Florida State University. By that time, I had lost my job and insurance, so the free program was a Godsend.

I watched behind two-way mirrors. I listened. I learned. I watched the repetitive words. I watched formation of movement of tongue and mouth, and single word production. Two semesters, one or two times a week, fifty miles one way to FSU, with little progress beyond single words. The instructor wanted him to have a Linquista machine to replace his speech. Or at least assist him with speech. I refused because to get a replacement for his speech would allow him to regress and not move forward. Also, the machine was very expensive.

I looked for more aggressive methods of speech therapy. Our youngest daughter had returned to South Florida. She learned of an aggressive program in speech, occupational, and physical therapies. I rented a motel room for a month in Naples, Florida. I took him to therapies. All therapies were aggressive, except speech. The lady in charge of aggressive speech therapy went on vacation after completing his first session. Every speech session thereafter started with a new student therapist. Each started the same way-just as they did at FSU. By the fourth week, progress was limited and frustrating. The last day, the new therapist began with, "I am so impressed." An hour later she was still saying "I am so impressed." She said it so much I wanted to throw-up.

We returned home to North Florida. I began my own speech therapy program of repetitive sentences. No single words. Repetitive usable sentences. Repetitive sentences he could use to ask for things. Repetitive sentences to tell doctors or me what hurts. He made up repetitive sentences like "My titties hurt." After which he would laugh and laugh. I worked with him every day. Everyday improvements for months. I constantly demanded he talk in sentence format. No charades. By watching professional speech therapists, I learned it was harder for him to retrieve single words. It was easier to say a simple repetitive sentence. He improved until I began working on my master's classes and I stopped regular practice. And he? He refused to practice by himself or with me when I had time.

I was tired of playing charades. I am tired of playing charades. I know people think I am cruel for demanding sentences. No! I am not. He needed sentences to talk to the few people who stopped by. He always talked non-stop. Total motor-mouth. His favorite expression has always been, "I was vaccinated with a Victrola needle." To require less effort from him allowed for defeat.

Two years after leaving Naples, Florida and non-aggressive speech therapy, we returned to give it another chance at success. Same company-different location. My daughter volunteered to keep him in her home and take him to therapies. He was eager to go to therapy and demanded to go three days a week. By the third or fourth week the occupational therapist gave up. He began physical therapy cooperatively and decreased in participation by the fifth month. At home his physical activity was non-existent and he sat in the wheelchair. Our daughter was becoming frustrated with his refusal to participate in his recovery. She had joined my club of frustration.

Speech therapy was a different ball game. I had hope. I took my repetitive sentence work sheets to the Naples speech therapist. I explained the progression and interruption. The speech therapist said she would review them. Whether she did or not is evident by the lack of progress with no advancement in speech. Apparently, she went to the same old routine of single words. By the fifth month she told my daughter he needed a Linquista machine and she was going to order him one. When my daughter called and said the speech therapist had ordered the machine, I protested. "He will not use the machine. It is a waste of money."

By the time I arrived back in Naples before Christmas, he had the machine a couple of weeks. He did not use it. He showed it off. He showed the machine's depiction of body parts naming the genitals. When he repeated the words the machine said, he said them distortedly. But mostly he laughed at the genitals. Then the machine sat in the corner collecting dust. As it does now.

I changed my psychology master's thesis research to effective therapies for Aphasia. I discovered aggressive speech therapy in combination with the Alzheimer's drug Namenda was producing dramatic results even for those aphasic patients who were eleven years post-stroke. I got him a prescription for **Namenda** and my daughter started him on the meds. He would be at maximum Namenda dosage for speech therapy when I arrive. I was ready. He was medically ready. I was hopeful.

I arrived just before Christmas. The meds were at maximum dosage. I sat down with him to begin the speech sessions. Hope for recovery was within reach. Or so I thought. I began the session. He refused to respond above a whisper. I responded with "louder". He responded with a whisper. Repeatedly, I demanded louder. The stroke voice is immature. He does not like the sound of his stroke voice. Therefore, he does not want to talk. Louder voice response brings back his true adult voice. Again, I demanded louder. He did respond. He responded with a scream, rage, and throwing things. I responded with a complete withdrawal. No more of wasting my time. No more wasting money on two-hundred-dollar prescription refills. I took him home.

At home, I decided to give it one more try, I hired a high school senior boy to stop by after school and use my speech protocol of repetitive sentences. It worked. He was excited to see the student. The student also added a few new sentences. This worked well as long as the student was in the house. But, when the student graduated, my husband stopped any attempt to talk except with charades. I gave up. Less stress on me.

=9=

WALKING LESSONS

When I lost my job and insurance, I applied for my husband to receive care from the Veteran's Clinics. He was turned down. When I received the denial letter, I drove my husband to Tallahassee, Florida VA clinic. I went in to talk to the two social workers. I told them to come out to the car and see this man I had no insurance to care for him. They refused to see him. But they immediately gave him medical rights for everything.

CHP never gave my husband a brace to walk. They gave him a Hemi-walker to use with his left hand. The VA gave him a brace all the way to his hip.   It was impossible to put on. Mostly he did not want it on because it was impossible to use. He used his left hand to move the Hemi-walker and he walked with the heavy VA brace on his right leg. It made him walk like a movie monster walking.

During the Naples, Florida aggressive therapies he walked. Three times per week he walked with the VA hip brace around an area the size of half a basketball court. The Naples, Florida therapist ordered a knee-high brace to replace the clumsy hip brace. He received it our last week in Naples. The knee-high brace was easier to use and easier to put on him. But it was up to him to use it after we left Naples. He rarely does. He likes his victim status.

When I take him to doctor's appointments, I make him wear the brace. I had got a scooter so that I could get him out of the house easily. But with the new brace and hemi walker, I made him walk up the ramp into the house. He refuses to walk down the ramp.

=10=

THE HANDICAP RAMP

In 1999, I inherited a little house which has a value less than the national poverty level. The Nine hundred square feet, house has a porch which extends across the front of the house; a little ramp sloped off the porch. The house's only occupant was a one-legged little old Black lady, who had lived in the little house for eight years. The house was not of much value, but the occupant was a real treasure.

Several months after inheriting the house, I discovered an elaborate "J" shaped handicap ramp attached to the porch. The ramp formed a pathway south twelve feet, turned east twenty feet, turned north and descended forty-five (clearly one-half the length of the house). Although the handicap ramp was a work of engineering artistry, the designer was a mystery.

One month after beginning work at the Taylor County Senior Center, an invoice for a three-thousand-dollar handicap ramp appeared on my desk. "The handicap ramp" attached to my inherited house. My boss did not know I owned the house. Being curious, I asked my boss a generic question about placement of handicap ramps on rental properties. "Does the Senior Center asks a landlord's permission before placement of handicap ramps on rental property occupied by center clients?"

The response was "No, landlords might refuse placement." I, having some legal training, clearly recognized this as an illegal encroachment on private property. But my lips were sealed. Hey! The ramp was worth almost as much as the house.

Fast forward to 2004, my husband's stroke. He was in the hospital four months. I did not know the extent of his condition mainly because our questions went unanswered. We did not know if he could or could not walk. He was drugged. So, no he really couldn't. We knew he had some problem with his right hand and with talking with or without a tube down his throat.

A wheelchair was ordered by CHP and he was wheeled around TMH rehab in it.

There was no way we could get my husband into our house without a ramp. I had a bright idea. We could move a portion of the inherited house's handicap ramp to my house. The lady had died and it was no longer needed there. The "J" shaped ramp was in sections and therefore could be disassembled and moved. Easily?

My idea was to disassemble the ramp by first removing the upper planks and then removing the under lying braces. All to be reassembled at my house. I did not write out instructions for my youngest daughter and my oldest daughter and her husband. I was not there when the deconstruction began. I believe it was Captain Kangaroo who said, "Put on your thinking caps before you do something." I don't think they put on theirs before attacking the project.

It makes me tired just thinking about all the work they did to move that ramp. My oldest daughter, her husband, and youngest daughter moved that ramp. They worked hard. They disconnected two sections in whole pieces. "Whole pieces". They struggled moving the two several hundred-pound sections to my house. They (three people) lifted the sections without heavy equipment. It makes me tired just remembering and writing about their struggle. But their labor's end result was great. The ramp was perfect. Steep, but perfect.

I brought my husband home, fortunately he had lost over one hundred pounds or I would not have been able to move him up the steep handicap ramp. My youngest daughter helped pull and push the man up and down the ramp until she returned to her job in another city. Then it was up to me to get the man up and down the steep ramp.

That is when my adventures with the handicap ramp began in full force. My husband began to gain weight and with each pound the pushing and pulling him up and down the ramp became harder. I explored many options from a pulley to hoist him up the ramp or a fork lift. Each idea brought new obstacles.

The handicap ramp versus the woman contest began in earnest. I decided that ramp was not going to defeat me. Pushing or pulling the man and his wheelchair up the steep ramp beginning at the foot of the ramp was getting more impossible for me. A new plan of action needed to be tried. The strategy: move the car from the driveway and run up the ramp. Okay. Good plan. I would run the husband filled wheelchair up the steep ramp. Yeah! The plan would work.

The plan in action: (1) I moved my husband and his wheelchair (no foot rest attached) next to the road, twenty feet from bottom of ramp. (2) Husband lifts feet. (3) I brace myself. (4) Ready. Set. Go. We're off. I begin the running push of the wheelchair like a horse out of the racing stall. Faster, faster, closer, ever closer to that steep handicap ramp. Round one. Woman won. Yeah! I hoped no one had a video camera to record us running up the ramp. All I needed was to see us on America's Funniest Videos.   I am sure we would have won the $100,000 prize.

I repeated the ramp run many times. My husband continued to gain weight and I moved to the opposite side of the road before being the run. Then it happened. Ready, set, go worked well until the front wheels of the wheelchair (which had turned the wrong direction) hit the bottom of the ramp. Pow! Out he flew. If only he had had wings. Evil Knevil he was not. He landed on the ramp bottom. Wheelchair on top of him. I landed on the back of the wheelchair. I hope that video camera was not around. If it was, it was a sure-fire winner of the $100,000 prize.

I removed the wheelchair off my husband and untangled him. There was no way I could pick him up. Where is that Wonder Woman strength when I need it? I ran across the street to an office where two men worked and asked them to help. The men picked him up, put him in the wheelchair and pushed him up the ramp into the house. The handicap ramp won this time.

I bought a scooter for my husband to ride up and down that ramp. That handicap ramp was not going to defeat me again.

The scooter allowed my husband to ride down the ramp safety. But I always looked for ways to make him independent. I refused to allow him to ride the scooter up the ramp. He had to walk. He wore the leg brace on some outings. With the use of the Hemi-walker and his brace, he was able to walk to the ramp. He would walk to the ramp, then immediately place the walker around his neck and pull himself up the ramp. Of course, that was it. As soon as he reached the backdoor, he was ready to sit in that wheelchair.

=11=

TRAVELING

My car blew up in August of 2004. I rented a van so that we could look for a new car. But, most importantly, we were taking our youngest daughter to Jacksonville, Florida for an interview to be on "The Apprentice". The weather became horrible about an hour away. The rain was pelting the windshield so hard, I could barely see. My husband had been off psychotropic drugs since March 2004, he has no problem with cognition. He just can't get words to his mouth. But when he grabbed the steering wheel, all hell broke loose. I was trying to keep us on the road. Screaming at him to turn loose. Hitting his hand on the wheel. Finally, he relented. We arrived in one piece. We survive our first trip.

You may ask, why not put him in the back seat? That would create a whining protest from him. The back seats do not recline. He demands the back of his seat reclined slightly.

Our level headed daughter did not make the cut for "The Apprentice." Following the round table interviews. She said, she "felt they were looking for loudmouths that wanted to argue rather than work.

Our first trip was only a prelude for future events. Several more times he grabbed the wheel. He was admonished that he would be sitting in the back seat if he touched the wheel again. He did not touch the wheel for some time. But the last time he touched the wheel, was the last. I believe he learned his lesson.

In 2007, we were headed from Naples, Florida to St. Petersburg, Florida, a two-and-a-half-hour trip. He decided he had to stop to pee. We had already done this once. But, before Sarasota, he saw a MacDonald's sign and demanded to stop. He does not have dementia, Parkinson's or Alzheimer's. Like children he throws tantrums when he doesn't get what he wants. I am driving at a speed near eighty. I am in the fourth lane next to the inside median. A line of three cars next to me. Nose to nose we are racing down the highway. I am moving forward. Cars are shifting lanes behind me. One following on my bumper.

"No, you have already stopped." I exclaimed. But that did not stop him. Four lanes of traffic and he grabs the steering wheel. Four lanes of traffic and those behind us did not know I had their lives in my hands. Not to mention my own.

Holding tight to the steering wheel, I look in the rearview mirror to see tailgaters, to the right three lanes of cars and trucks matching my speed. He begins pulling the wheel right into the other lanes while I am pulling in the opposite direction toward the median. I began screaming at him. Then I began pounding his arm to let loosen his grip on the wheel. It seemed like an eternity. When he let loose, he began pounding my right upper arm. Over and over, he pounded.

I screamed, "I am calling the police". I called 911. He started pouting. I pulled off interstate 75 and stopped at a convenience store just before the sheriff officer arrived. They gave him a scolding and took him to the men's restroom. Where I had to rescue him. He can't get out with a right-hand grab bar. The officers wanted him to sit in the back, but the car was loaded. As a retired sheriff department officer, he was embarrassed.

He behaves now, but when we have to travel, I remind him that I will call police if he grabs the wheel. So far, he has not grabbed it again. My arm hurt for weeks-deep inside, from the pounding that day.

Traveling with him is worse than pulling teeth without drugs. If he sees a sign for a rest area or MacDonald's he will demand to stop, even if he had gone a short time before. This makes me angry and tired. We had left my sister's house in Navarre, Florida and had gone only twenty miles before he is demanding to stop. I stopped unloaded the wheelchair, pulled him out, wheeled him inside for tinkle. Loading him and the wheelchair back into the car, away we go. Although, I bought a PT Cruiser into which a wheelchair can be easily placed, when you add luggage and pack it in, it is a real chore to make stops. Another hour later, he started again. This time I reached behind the seat and pulled out a plastic urinal and handed to him. That made him mad. He finally pulled down the front of his pull-on shorts and popped his penis and balls into the urinal. There he sat penis and balls hanging out in the jug for almost two hours. Five miles from home he puts the urinal down, pulls up his shorts. I knew he didn't need to pee. Upon telling about this funny event, our sons-in-law responded, "It is hard to pee sitting down." It is not hard for him because he has been doing it since his stroke.

Traveling-driving in itself is pleasurable and therapeutic to me. When I am alone! But with my husband…you never know what to expect. Except that you are going to haft to stop and go to the bathroom multiple times. A one-hour trip ends with demanding bathroom visit before appointments. An hour and a half drive require one stop, sometimes two. That means I am going to swing his wheelchair in and out of the car many times. His original chair was very heavy; therefore, I took an Olympic discus stance from right to left and fling the chair into the back of the vehicle. Pulling muscles and creating exhaustion. Getting the chair out was not as stressful; I just needed to raise it high enough not to scratch the paint on the vehicle.

Staying in motels and hotels are a test of my endurance. More like a night or two in a torture chamber. No matter what I check into there is always a complaint from him. The furniture is to close; the beds are too close together; the toilet is a little low, and the list goes on. Although he may not be very verbal, he gets his message across with charades, hand jesters and tantrums.

I needed to give him a bath and I checked into a Hampton Inn somewhere west of Marianna, Florida. It was their handicapped room; a tub with lots of grab bars. He took one look and refused because the tub side was high, he would have to stand up, no shower bench. Oh well, no bath.

It is hard to move furniture in motel/hotel rooms, some beds are secured to the floor. The night stand between beds is always in his way. He has to compromise, which he does not like. In front of the nightstand, he sits arranging his two urinals, a stack of paper napkins, his glasses, and his watch. When he is secure on the bed, he again positions the urinals.

During the early months after stroke, I had to repeat instructions (even at home) so that he will properly seat himself on the bed. By that I mean, he will stand up, turn himself and sit on the edge of the bed. If he does not sit close to the nightstand, he will not be able to reach the headboard and pull himself onto the bed. When he is finally positioned on the bed, I move the wheelchair from between the beds. I turn the wheelchair around and back it next to the bed. The wheelchair in place allows him to pull himself up to get out of bed. He always lies on the left side of the bed with his right immobile arm next to the edge.

=12=

ACCESSIBILITY

Although, I am fully aware that handicap accessible laws are in effect, I never really noticed them until forced too. Restaurants, restrooms in any facility including civic centers, hotels, and motels are accessible? In some degree. Checking into hotels or motels, I now ask to see the rooms before checking in. The outside may have handicap accessible signs and sloped walk ways. It does not mean that the building itself is accessible.

Medieval Times in Orlando, Florida is a perfect example of failure to adapt to accessibility laws. Our youngest daughter had arranged a birthday celebration for her son and her father at Medieval Times. There was no elevator. Upon arriving, I noticed a very extremely steep pathway from ground to second floor. I assumed they must direct the horses through that entry. Unfortunately, when handicap individuals were instructed to follow a young lady, we were escorted outside to the base of the steep pathway and told to proceed upward. A power wheelchair could not maneuver the ramp. If I had been alone, there would have been no party attendance. My oldest and middle daughter's husbands and my youngest daughter's friend pushed that wheelchair bound man up that incline. One slip from either would have caused all three to plummet to ground. Exiting was same scenario. But we also had to consider the wheelchair escaping their grasp and rolling over everyone. With possible death injury and a lawsuit in tow.

Eating out can be a problem. When I find a restaurant which meets our needs and treats us with respect, I try to make sure that all meals are taken there. I take my husband to restaurants where the waiters have treated my husband with respect. At a small restaurant called Anthony's, in Tallahassee, Florida even the restaurant owner would come out and greet us as friends. Many times, we had the same waiter and he always remembered what my husband ordered. Always the same. I do not order it. I make him say it. He wants Mama's meatballs. Always, with lots of cheese. I also give the credit card to my husband so that he can hand it to the waiter anywhere we go.

I am always puzzled by restaurant and building doors. They have handicap ramps, why then are their doors so impossibly heavy? Normally when I arrive at a door, I must swing his chair around and pull him into the building while bracing the door with my body. While on the issue of doors, I wonder why there is a necessity to have double entry doors divided by a small foyer. The small foyers are usually filled with some décor which prevents easy turn around or pulling second door open without hitting the wheelchair. It couldn't possibly be to prevent flies. As I have been to some where there were flies inside.

Outback Steak House is great. But they have huge wooden doors that are heavy for one person to pull. But try pulling it open and pulling a wheelchair inside. It is hard work. Sometimes the hostess may notice and open the door. Sometimes not. We have been to a number of restaurants with similar heavy doors. All a struggle. Sometimes patrons assist with our entry and we never forget to say thank you.

I also wonder why the Federal government would rent a building for veteran's medical services without examining entry doorways. The Tallahassee Veteran's Clinic rents a building where the double door foyer is only large enough for a wheelchair. That means that both doors must be open before a wheelchair can enter. Other rented Veteran's buildings have manual doors which must be braced open to pull the wheelchair inside. Oh well, we the caregivers must adapt.

Restaurant restrooms are a challenge. When my children were little, we called them restroom inspectors. They were always polite, but they had to inspect the restroom. My husband has become the restroom inspector. Never fails. I have to check the lady's restroom for anyone inside. Coast clear, in he goes. Easy enough if there is a left-hand grab bar. If not a real struggle to maneuver the wheelchair begins. The wheelchair has to be moved so that he can use the chair to balance, sit and pull up. One bar-b-cue restaurant in Chiefland, Florida had a bathroom doorway so small that I had to leave his wheelchair blocking the door and walk him, without brace and hemi-walker, into the restaurant restroom about ten feet.

We have gone on a few trips and I had to carry the stinky raised toilet seat along. But I never take it inside a restaurant. Only motel/hotel rooms. I wrapped the stinky seat in garbage bags. Dragging your plastic toilet seat into motels is not fun. Once we stayed for a month in a motel handicapped room, I had to buy a new seat because the motel toilet opening was too small for our plastic seat. I also bought a shower head extension to give my husband a bath. Their adaption of handicap laws consisted of attaching grab bars in the tub area and an exterior ramp. But this is a common practice in many motels and hotels. Especially in older ones.

Some newer hotels and motels have several grab bars around the tub. I suppose to prevent any accident scenario. But it still is a tub with grab bars. Tubs present a challenge for those with stroke related leg and arm paralysis. Not to mention any other debilitating disease.

In Palm Beach, Florida I stopped at a big hotel without checking the room. I checked in, pushed him into the room. There in the bathroom, I found a right-side grab bar, which I could have maneuvered. He really needs left hand grab bar. But attached to the wall was a metal towel rack. A metal towel rack placed at such a position that if my husband tried to stand up from the toilet, his head would ram into the metal rack. I checked out. Hazard avoided. I drove across town to Palm Beach, located a Best Western. I looked at the room. A dump it was; a make shift grab bar was mounted into floor of bathroom. Oh, Hell! I wanted to go back to the nice hotel. But we stayed because he was agitated. Thirty minutes later my husband had to pee. Then it was too late to check out. My husband's wheelchair could not get pass furniture to the bathroom. I moved furniture.

At a Best Western motel in Naples, Florida things were perfect. Two beds, roll-in shower, left-handed grab bar and tall toilet. Perfect? No. The non-adjustable tub bench was child size. He threw a fit about it being low. I had to use a lot of strength to pull him up. Next time I brought a large bench.

I am not aware of the regulations within the handicap accessible guidelines for hcights of toilets or placement of grab gars. But invariably some hotels, restaurants, convention centers use child height toilets. These very low toilets mean I have to get in front of him and pull with all my might if I do not carry an adaption seat. I do not carry an adaption any longer. Away with those stinky things.

I have always asserted that men design bathrooms, especially bathroom stalls in public places. The paper holder is always in the way. This is also true of roll-in showers. Men design them. A motel in Naples, Florida removed their tub and without extending flooring-built a roll-in shower which is too small. Water flows all over the bathroom floor. An accident waiting to happen.

=13=

TANTRUMS

My youngest daughter's friend's father had a similar medical issue. The man had guns in his house. Rather than endure the illness, he killed himself. Therefore, my daughter was concerned about the guns which were in our house. I never liked guns and didn't want to see them in view. Over the years hunting guns were replace by pistols for transporting money from business to bank and some for-pistol training with the sheriff's department. So, as a preventive measure all guns were removed from our house. Removing guns from our house has not stopped his tantrum throwing displays of wanting to kill himself.

We moved to Naples, Florida, 2009, in hopes of me securing a job. My husband was in one of tantrums because I would not put on his right shoe. I had just given him a bath, dressed him-except for his shoes and socks. He wanted expensive Crocs shoes which are easy for him to put on. He has Croc shoes. He can put them on. Shoes and socks are his responsibility. It was easier for him to put on the shoe when he was thinner, now his belly makes it a harder. It is his only job. He can do it. I will not.

Our fifteen-year-old grandson had arrived during his tantrum. Our grandson told him, "Papa, you can do it." Our grandson then walked away. My husband again starts pleading with me to put on the shoe. We were temporarily renting a home with a sunken living room. He can't reach me. In the sunken living room, our grandson sat in a chair thirteen-feet from his grandfather. I sat on the sofa eleven-feet from my husband and his tantrum.

There he was throwing a tantrum for his grandson to witness. There the man sat in his wheelchair, his face red with anger. In rage he raised the Hemi-walker in his left hand over and over. Then the man threw it. I know he meant to hit me. I should have told my grandson to go to another room. But I didn't think the jerk would throw the walker or throw it that far. The walker flew thirteen-feet and landed on the floor next to my shocked grandson Our shocked grandson jumped up and ran out the front door. He was calling his mother. She promptly came to the house and scolded her father. He could have hurt his grandson. Our grandson had heard of the tantrums. This was his first time witnessing it.

When the walker did not hit me and our grandson ran out the front door, my husband went to the sliding glass door to the pool area. He pulled and pulled. But the door would not open. He was going to roll his chair out into the pool. If he had succeeded in opening the door, I would not have stopped him from rolling out. The hateful man put on his shoe.

Once In Naples, Florida we stayed at the Gulf Coast Inn which had a roll-in shower. But I had to share a bed with him. We had stayed several times. The last time, I checked out at 3:45 am because he was driving me insane. We were leaving anyway, but I was not leaving until seven hours later. When we have to share a bed, I sleep with my head at his feet because he takes most of the bed. I usually wake every two hours. But this night was like no other. It was the night from Hell. He went to sleep at eleven.

I wake every two hours and must get out of bed are I will not go back to sleep. When I sleep in the same bed with him, I do not reach deep sleep. I took my bath, two muscle relaxers to help me sleep and I got into bed. Then he started. Every thirty minutes he popped up and sat on the side of the bed. I am getting angrier every minute. Then I am hollering. By 2 am I was ready to push his half-naked T-shirt clad body out the door and leave him there. I held back, only because he would have made such a racket that I would probably have been arrested for abuse. Again, to bed.

I was furious at 3:45 am when he sat on the side of bed. Then I am really hollering. I am louder. That gets my forty plus years of marriage to a jackass into a boiling tantrum and I let him have it with both barrels. I could get my children from a sperm bank. No house for our family. Reason for my tantrum started in full force.

I threw everything in the car, dressed his hateful self-centered self, loaded his butt and wheelchair and off to checkout. I am sleepy from the muscle relaxers. But I am going to drive this jackass five and a half hours home. I had to beat on the door to wake the front desk clerk who was asleep on lobby sofa. When my youngest daughter called around 9:00 am, I am half asleep behind the wheel. My words to her were: "If I have a wreck and I die and this man survives, you remind him that it is his fault." Then I gave her a description of my horrible night.

I hear endless remarks about the "terrible two's". My children never entered a phase like that until their teens. But to have a sixty-plus year-old man, behave like a two-year-old is disgusting.

But there he is behaving like a two-year-old and many times like he is retarded. That to me is embarrassing. He is not retarded. But he will act like it.

Over the past eight years, my husband has swung at me many times. Sometimes he has landed a few. But I am not the only one to view his rage. My youngest daughter was taking him for therapies in Naples, Florida. He had been getting more and more uncooperative with therapy. Then it happened. He raised his hand to her while she was driving. She responded with, "I'm not twelve anymore, and I will get out and beat your ass if you hit me." She stopped him in midair. And so, it goes. Are we having fun yet?

=14=

QUIRKS

Quirks. He has quirks! Two washcloths for bathing-one for bathing and one for wiping his eyes. I will never understand a grown man wiping his eyes with a dry washcloth and with the same washcloth wipe the edges of his face-next to fully foamed shampooed hair-cloth picking up shampoo as it moves and then, and then re-wiping his eyes, while the gathered shampoo smears onto his eyelids. I take the shampoo encrusted washcloth away from him. I take another washcloth and clean up his mess. Women have more brains!

Quirks. He has quirks! He has four or five combs. Each comb just like the other. In our Perry house, when I have given him a bath and comb his hair afterwards-I clean the comb before using it. But in the Naples, Florida house, I needed to trim his neck hairline, when finished I placed the dirty comb and scissors inside the side door next to his outside bath area. All the things I must do to unravel the outside shower preparations takes time. I did not pick up the scissors and comb because I was busy picking up washcloths, towel, and sheets on the outside of the house. I will pick up scissors and comb when I am ready. But every time I am in the middle of something he starts about that stupid damn comb. He can't get it because he can't step down into the den.

Quirks. He has quirks! In the Naples house, although the dresser is only inches from the bathroom door, about eight pm, he removes his shorts for the next day and places them on the sink counter six feet away. He also tucks a small towel into the handrail near the toilet. At eleven pm, he sits on the toilet, removes the small towel from the handrail-folding it in half and places it in a specific location in the wheelchair seat. At bedside, upon getting out of the wheelchair, he moves the folded towel back to the specific location in the seat.

Quirks. He has quirks! Bedtime is quirk time. He always heads to bed at eleven every night. When I am busy, I do not notice the time or his disappearance to bathroom. He goes to the bathroom and starts hollering my name. He always leaves for the bathroom before the last scene of any television program I am watching. I think he plans it that way.

Quirks. He has quirks! The pillow and the hospital bed hand buttons must be in a specific spot-hand button on top back edge of the pillow-pillow exact middle. If not, I get the demanding charades. To get into bed, he pulls his wheelchair at an angle about half-way along the side of the bed. There he brakes both sides of the chair and tries to stand up. In order to rise from the chair, he must first push his right foot closer to the edge of the chair's front right wheel. Second, he must slide forward in wheelchair to gain his balance. If he does not slide forward in the chair, he will not have the needed balance to stand. When seated on the bed, he repositions the small towel on the seat of the chair and unlocks brakes of chair-he moves the wheelchair almost to the foot end of the bed and locks the right-side brake only. From this position he cannot reach left brake. In the morning, he raises the bed head which forces him lower in the bed-he swings his feet over the side of bed and reaches to unlock right chair brake and pulls chair forward. He reaches over and locks both brakes and gets into the chair. If I am not up by eight-thirty every morning, he is hollering my name.

Quirks. He has quirks! In our Perry house the handicap ramp is very steep. Although a carpenter adjusted the lower part of the ramp, it is still steep. I purchased a scooter to get my husband in and out to the house. Because he refuses to walk with his brace for exercise, I must find some method of movement which forces him to use his muscles. Before we leave the house, I put his right leg brace and shoes on. I help him get onto the scooter and away he goes. After loading him into the car, I drive the scooter back into the house. Upon our return, I give him the hemi-walker and make him walk up the ramp. It is not something he wants to do. When he reaches the handicap ramp, I usually take the walker and place it at the backdoor. Using the ramp rail, he pulls himself up the ramp to the back door. There he takes the hemi-walker and goes through the door and stops in the kitchen. There he stands demanding his wheelchair, which I had removed from the car and parked further in the house. He is too lazy to walk further. Sometimes, when I do not take the hemi-walker at the beginning of the ramp, he will hang the hem-walker around his neck and walk up the handicap ramp. He also does this when we go to the doctor's office. He looks silly with the walker hanging from his neck. In the Naples house there is no ramp, just a two inch step up. He won't walk from the car to the door. I have to push the husband loaded wheelchair to the door, swing chair around and pull him over the step up.

Quirks. He has quirks! My husband has issues with car seats. His car seat back must be reclined a little. Although no one adjusts it or rarely anyone sits in the seat except him, he always has a complaint. Using charades, he motions back of seat be moved. "No one has sat in the seat." I declare. But that is not sufficient, I must adjust it. He gets out of the wheelchair and sits in the car seat. I must then pick up his right brace encased leg and move it into car. Immediately he starts complaining-his leg is not in right position-the seat back is not in correct position. Here we go again-making adjustments; bring seat back into the original position.

Quirks. He has Quirks! When the Scot's brand disposable wipes began airing commercials, he wanted some. The television commercials for Scot's disposable wipes have indoctrinated him. I have bought other brands-none were satisfactory to him. He demands Scot's.

Quirks. He has quirks! Before the surgery and stroke-he wore baggy boxer underwear. Baggy underwear-just like his baggy pants. I like a man to wear a pair of pants. I do not like to see a man wear pants that look like another person could get in there with them. Elvis Presley or Tom Jones black leather pants. Elvis or Tom Jones or anyone else who wears a pair of pants well-where are you? Oh! Dream on. Baggy underwear disappeared after the surgery. He uses two bedside urinals at night; he does not like underwear because they get in the way. He has not worn underwear-baggy or otherwise since the surgery-2003. That in and of itself is not an issue. Going out in public-in shorts with no underwear is a problem. He refuses to wear long pants. I have repeatedly reminded him to make sure his penis and balls are not flopping out for all to see.

Quirks. He has quirks! He has always had a quirk for two pocket shirts. Two pockets to put things in. Two pockets-not nerdy-just two pockets. Drives us all crazy. He does not want anything but two pocket shirts. Well, the stroke fixed that; he wears what I buy him. Although he refuses any pull over shirts, except T-shirts for bed. Drives me crazy.

Quirks. He has quirks! Several times I have taken him to lunch or dinner at restaurants and he has acted like a moron. "You are not stupid, so stop acting like it." I demanded. People look at us in revulsion. I look at a parent with a child, who has MS or some other debilitating disease, and pity them for their burden. I do not look at them with revulsion. It embarrasses me when my husband behaves as a child and people look at me with pity and revulsion.

I do not take my husband out to eat in our home town of Perry, because he acts retarded and people looked repelled. In the beginning of recovery, when he met someone, he knew before the surgery he would holler, start crying, and kiss their hands. The people were surprised and did not know how to deal with his behavior. I would reassure them everything was okay. I no longer take him out any place in Perry.

=15=

THE HYPOCHONDRIAC

Never, ever let a hypochondriac hear a sniffle, a cough, and especially a diagnosis of brain aneurism. I had spent years ignoring the exaggerated sniffles, coughs, and feigned illness of this man. He was convinced he had a brain tumor. He had had bad headaches since before we were married. They became so bad that he arranged for a visit the Mayo Clinic in Rochester, Minnesota. Our middle daughter was an infant when we went. The clinic found nothing. He is a hypochondriac. Years later a chiropractor in Lakeland, Florida, said the headaches were a response to bones shifting due to a car wreck when he was an infant. Facial manipulation reduced the instance of headaches to almost zero.

I trained my children not to cough, sneeze, or sniffle around him. It encourages a new illness in him. My parents scolded me many times for not paying attention to his faked illnesses. "He is a hypochondriac. He is not sick." I explained to deaf ears. They pitied him because I would not listen. I lived with him; I knew him better than they did.

I told him repeatedly, "If you cry wolf long enough, eventually you're going to get caught." Years later, he had heart surgery and an on-demand pacemaker put in. All because of weight issues and too many prescription drugs for feigned illnesses.

I did not realize he was getting pills from doctors by the armful. While he was four months in the hospital, I was clearing his room to prepare for his arrival home. I discovered he had three drawers filled with prescription drugs. All kinds of drugs for his faked illnesses. But one bottle intrigued me more than the other. A bottle of methadone. Methodone? Methodone is usually used as part of a drug addiction detoxification program. Okay, he was a prescription addict also. I didn't know.

I never bought his medicine. I did not know what he was taking. I prefer to have a lucid brain-not a drug induce state of being. Although now that I look back at the years flown by with no change of anything constructive or gained from marriage to this man, I should have been drugged.

He refuses to put on his brace. He refuses to walk. He refuses recovery because it would remove his excuse. On September 30, 2009, I took him to the Naples, Florida Veteran's Clinic for an exam. The doctor said, "If he doesn't want too. Don't make him. Your life will be easier." Yeah, right! My life would be easier... Fill in the blank. It will not be easier until... Fill in the blank. Where's his lolly-pop, doctor?

In 2011, he had a toothache. We had a devil of a time getting anyone to pull the tooth in Naples, Florida. The dentist all wanted me to take him to an oral surgeon. Oral surgeon to pull a tooth. I took him to a dentist in Fort Myers, Florida. They wanted to discuss pulling the tooth with the VA doctor. We don't have money or insurance to screw around with that crap. I told the dentist that.

My husband starts a tantrum and throws a fit. He is slashing out at me because I don't have money or insurance. Pulls himself up out of the dental chair and demands his wheelchair. Out he goes. Outside I'm throwing my own tantrum as he swings at me. I was supposed to get him lunch. But damned if I'm going to feed him.

Oral Gel is what he gets for his tooth. Weeks later, he starts again. But this time I found a "normal" dentist who will pull the tooth. The tooth was very long so they gave him a child's medal for the longest tooth. If you act like a child, you will be treated like a child.

=16=

FRIENDS

Friends? My husband thought he had a lot of friends. If he did, they were fair weather friends. If he did, they were friends until they borrowed money from him and disappeared forever on the day, they were to pay him back. If he did, they were friends in lip service only.

I had a teacher in the sixth grade, named Mr. Bryant. It must have been his first year as a teacher, I don't know. But he made a statement to me that I shall never forget. He said, "Friends are people who visit your house. If they don't, they are not your friends." Following his statement, I only have three or four friends. Apparently, my husband has none-now. Two older

friends have died since my husband's stroke. Of the other's he thought were friends, where are

they?

He was friends with a married couple-older than he. They visited three times in the first few

years. They must drive in front of our house to visit their relatives. Once I caught them driving

slowly beside my house. I went to the front door to greet them. They did not stop-just turn the

corner and drove away. A few weeks later, she called. I told her I had gone to the front door to

meet them. She sputtered making excuses. The wife calls about every ten months. The last time

I told her, "I did not like people calling up asking about him and never coming to see him."

These people he has known from school-a long time, ago.

Now, I understand that people do not like to see people, around their own age, who are sick or

disabled. It puts the reality of life's limit in their face. It could be them instead of him in that

wheelchair. Better you than me in that wheelchair. There, but for the grace of God-go I. Yep! I

understand.

For years I watched my husband visit his friends. They rarely returned the visits. For years I

watched one couple call my husband to verify gossip around town. If he didn't know it, he

would find out the truth. I watched. I mentioned it to my youngest daughter. She watched.

Then my husband retired. Then my husband had that damn surgery which gave him a stroke.

He can no longer find truth about gossip. He cannot gossip. He cannot talk, but in short

sentences. They no longer come by and rarely call. What a shame.

We had a little friend, Miss Betty, who turned eighty-nine, October 2010. She came every day to our home in Perry. Almost every day she brought him flowers. Every day she watched him bury his nose in the flowers-sniffing everyone. Every day she sat with me.

Our angel needed me, as much as I needed her to listen to my trials of caregiving. She was a caregiver to her husband. He was big-like my husband. She is short like me. She struggled and no one knew how hard it was for her to care for him. She understands the frustration. My husband has limited speech and walking ability because he refuses to participate in his recovery. Her husband could talk. But he could not walk. He had no choice. He had to lie in bed for five years. She understands. Do you understand the caregiver burden?

My husband said, "He never wanted to be a burden to anyone." But he is a burden. A heavy burden. I was shocked when Miss Betty told me that her remarks after her husband died were, "Free at last. Free at last. Thank God almighty, I'm free at last. Free at last." Although the words shocked me, I understood her relief from her burden.

Miss Betty was our little angel. Her car dashboard was covered with eighty-nine angels to guide her way. A policeman gave her a ticket for driving too slowly and having an angel obstructed view. He told her she needed to remove the angels. That made her unhappy. She has traveled all over the country with those angels on the dash. I told her to go see the judge. The judge told her, "You can never have too many angels." He dismissed her ticket.

In June 2011, our friend Betty Duvall died. I walked in her shoes. Sometimes we so easily go about our daily lives without a glancing thought to "WHO DID THAT?" At funerals of children some people say "We know how you feel." Without having lost a child. I was in line to comfort a grieving parent of his only child, when someone uttered those, "We know how you feel" words. The father responded, "NO YOU DON'T!" And that is no truer statement. If we have not walked in their shoes, we do not know.

Miss Betty's husband lay flat on his back for five years. For five years she cared for his every need. She got a waterbed so that it would be easier to turn him when giving him a bath. One day she bounced the bed just a little too hard. That man nearly flew off the bed. When she finally asked for help, the Florida state worker told them to get a divorce. Miss Betty's husband cried, "You wouldn't do that Momma would you?" She never did.

When Miss Betty's shadow fell upon my door eight years ago, there was no halo or large white fluttering wings. But, none the less she was an angel in disguise. When his friends stopped coming, Miss Betty stopped by almost every day. He laughed, like a three-year-old at Christmas when she brought him flowers or an elephant.

She understood the caregiver position, the isolation, and all the other feelings of the sole caregiver. She had been there. She was there for me. We had long talks. As the days passed into years she kept coming. Some days she was tired from her daily treks around town, taking smiles to everyone who needed them. She and I talked a while. When her talking slowed and her head bobbed little, I reduce my chatter and let her doze off. When she couldn't get up from soft furniture, she sat in a large rocking chair. When she dozed off, I let her rest. Only to wake her when she began tilting the rocking chair forward. I didn't want her to fall out of the chair.

Miss Betty, in her little red station wagon adorned with eighty-nine angels guiding her way was filled with stuff toys to hand to any child and buckets of flowers to give to shut-ins, had been sidelined for some time. A simple byline of her passing may be over looked by many, unknowing that they may have received from her giving spirit. I was not there when she became the caretaker of her baby sister, nor her brother's three small children, nor the many foster babies and young children in Michigan. I never knew how many foster children she cared for in Taylor County. But I heard it was around eighty before her husband became ill.

Miss Betty followed the biblical words of feeding the hungry and clothing the naked with her volunteer hours gathering clothes, filling and delivering food pantry bags to those in need. She never belonged to a club requiring community service. She was community service. She began making wreaths for the courthouse eternal flame without being asked. She never had to be asked to do anything. She never asked for help for herself.

When her house was unlivable, I helped her get into a senior living apartment. I had already given her a hospital bed so that she could get out of bed easier. I helped her sell a large car which was dangerous and hard for her to drive. I helped her find a small car similar to her original red wagon which was unrepairable.

So, who cared for Miss Betty in her new apartment? There are many who stopped in to check on her. Some stayed the night. All their names I do not know. I just know that we shall never have another so unselfishly giving in our county. Today, Miss Betty has her fluttering white wings and halo. And I. I have a hole in time to fill with her memory.

PART- 3

A NEW EXISTENCE

February 2010, I fell and broke my arm. I had to have help bathing my husband. The local senior services is impotent to deliver immediate service. This is partly because the state has taken control over delivery of service. I called the Tallahassee VA clinic and asked for help. They immediately arranged for bathers twice a week. Thank Heaven for them.

When my arm had healed, I had two bouts with pneumonia. The second time I waited three days with 104-degree temperature before calling the doctor. I spend three days in the hospital. That was the turning point for me. I needed help or I was going to land in a mental hospital.

I decided to place my husband in assisted living. I had asked a couple of people how they felt about putting their mothers in nursing homes. I started exploring. VA respite was only for thirteen days. I needed more.

I took my husband to visit the Shrine's Home in St. Petersburg, Florida. They were nice but very expensive. So, I looked at the Robert H. Jenkins, Jr. Veterans' Domiciliary in Lake City, Florida. It is run by the State of Florida. It was expensive also. The VA does not pay for it. We would be penniless. But it was a necessary evil.

I arranged for my husband to arrive the middle of June 2010. Because I do not have a way to move his power-chair, my youngest daughter came from Naples to move the chair to Lake City. We all arrived to find they were not ready for him. I had specifically asked that he have a left-hand grab bar in the bathroom. Not once, but several times. They assured me that they did and they were ready for him. But they were not.

I had to leave the powerchair in their care for a week. It was supposed to be locked away. It was not. When we arrived a week later, they brought the chair out to us. We protested the chair was not his. It was damaged, half of the right arm covering was ripped off and the toggle switch covering had been ripped off. He protested more. Then I remembered I had written his last four of social security number in the back pocket of the chair. There it was. They had done the damage. They did the damage, denied it and they never repaired it either.

Five weeks later, we removed my husband because they did not call us about his medical issues. My youngest daughter arrived in Lake City for a short visit. Only to find her father missing and no one could tell her where he was. Finally, someone said he was in the VA hospital down the street. He had been sent there three times that night because they couldn't his control fever. But mostly, she discovered he had Mersa Staph infection on his right leg.

My grandson and I saw my husband on July 5th, 2010. We stopped by on our adventure to see the United States together. My husband was fine. But five weeks later, we are on the way to Detroit and upper Michigan to see my cousin. When My daughter called hysterical. "He could die from Mersa. You need to come home." He was delusional because it was in his blood stream. She took pictures of the infection, talked to doctors waited for results and us to return to Florida.

I did not want to get on the plane to Florida. My grandson and I had been to Atlanta, New England, Niagara Falls and headed to upper Michigan. My cousin said, "It probably wasn't as bad as it seemed." But we had to make the detour. It wasn't as bad as it seemed when I arrived. But we removed all his belongings from the Jenkin's Domiciliary. He remained in the VA hospital for several more days, while arrangements could be made in Naples, Florida skilled nursing facility. He was moved to Naples where he stayed in skilled nursing another month. Followed by her caring for him with daily cleaning and dressing of the infected area for an additional three months. If she had not attended to these issues, he could have died from the neglect in Lake City.

But I, I returned to Detroit. My grandson had to stay with his mother for school to start. I alone flew back to Detroit and picked up my car to continue my adventure. Across the United States I drove. I wanted to make all lower forty-eight. I loved every second. But it wasn't long enough. A year later it seems as though it never happened.

I hope someday to have enough money to finish my trip. I only made thirty-eight states. Although, many have said I wasted my money on the trip. I respond, "It was cheaper than staying in the hospital with a nervous breakdown."

And for my husband, he was moved from skilled nursing to a private apartment. He has his own hospital bed, his own TV, and only a few of his two thousand plus elephants. The apartment has a roll-in shower and a left-hand grab bar by the toilet, a small sink and refrigerator. He is relatively content. He must interact with people. Interaction is something he has been lacking for years. Meals are served in the dining room and he must take his powerchair to get there. He has an assigned table with three ladies who are around ninety each. After some meals he will go outside and pick flowers to give to others.

To save money my daughter arranges his pills and gives him a bath twice a week. When I am in the area, I give him a bath. Every day one of us visits him. He does not want to go home. And me, I don't want him home. I am less stressed and my hair has stopped falling out. But I am broke because ninety-eight percent of our income goes to house him.

Part- 4

=1=

WHY THE HELL AM I SO ANGRY?

I hate caregiving. With a capital C period. Never asked for it. Never wanted it. But I am stuck. Recently I read an analogy of caregiving in which caregiving chores were compared to caring for a new puppy. Cleaning up dog poo is caregiving. Either way, it is shit and nobody wants the job.

October 16, 2009, University of Arkansas coach Frank Broyles' and his daughter and granddaughter appeared on the "Dr. Phil show". They had written a book called, "Broyles' Playbook for Alzheimer's Caregivers". The three people sat recounting events of caregiving they had experienced while caring for Mr. Broyles' wife. Simple tactics to keep her happy and content without frustration. They played a game of life which allowed all four to co-exist as her Alzheimer's disease progressed. They were supportive of each other in a loving environment. The Broyles' had a happy unit working together. I do not. What these people did and a desire to help others led them to write the book. That is great.

My husband does not have Alzheimer's! Therefore, that is not an excuse for his bad behavior. He has no excuse. He has always wanted his way or no way. I should have gone-away. How selfish and guilty I feel about resenting caring for him. But I should not be. I gave everything. He gave nothing. I resent having to care for him because I know he does not want to recover. I resent caring for him because he gave me nothing but children which I could have gotten from a sperm bank. The sperm bank donor promises nothing. I would not have wasted my life waiting for promises and fulfillment. I would not have seen the wasted potential of a man.

=2=

My father died at six p.m. on Christmas day 1998. My parents had been married fifty-seven years. He had cancer ten or twelve years before and they removed a portion of his lung. The cancer returned. It was terminal. A year of VA doctors playing games with his treatment. Six months began the downhill turn. Six weeks he became weaker. My mother began complaining. She wanted to put him in a nursing home. She didn't want to care for him. She was selfish.

My mother was about five-six and almost two hundred pounds. My father was about five-three, ninety-seven pounds and shrinking. During the last six weeks he used a wheelchair more than walked. My mother called my sister repeatedly about putting Daddy in a nursing home. He did not need to go. She just didn't want to care for him. Two weeks before Christmas, Hospice began visiting. Hospice gave my mother morphine. "To make him comfortable." She gave him morphine to a stupor state. He could not talk or do anything. I told her she was giving him too much of a dose. But she came back with, "They said to make him comfortable".

When a guy from Hospice came by her house, I was the first person he met. He asked me how Mother was doing. I told him the truth. Apparently, he doesn't expect or get the truth. I told him, "She is resentful". And she was. She resented caring for him. She just didn't want to be bothered.

Now, one could say I am acting the same way. But no, resentful I should be. I have good cause. My mother on the other hand should not be resentful. She was paid handsomely for his end-of-life care. My mother was married to my father fifty-seven years during which time she got five houses-one old house and four new houses with nobody's stink left in them. She got vacations every year. After Daddy's retirement she got a new car every year. She had five children and always worked out of the home. She was not a homemaker. She was not much of a mother either. Definitely not a grandmother to my children. She had favorites.

=3=

The wedding vows, "...to have and to hold from this day forward, for better or for worse, for richer, for poorer, in sickness and in health, to love and to cherish; from this day forward until death do us part." Who the Hell made up this crap? "....to have and to hold this day forward" gets a pass because translated it means you're stuck. "...for better or worse," well Hell where is the better? I have been damned with the worst for forty-two years. I guess I needed binoculars to find the better. "...for richer," well Hell, somebody forgot to tell the man this part or he was deaf. Richer never entered his mind and foreign to him. "...for poorer," we have been nothing but poor from day one. He strived for nothing more. "...in sickness and in health," well it does not mention one thing about hypochondriacs' feigned illnesses. As for the rest of the vows, they are an illusion.

My daughter insisted that her father needed anti-depressants. I took him to the VA in Tallahassee, Florida. They referred us to a VA psychologist, who in turn sent us to a psychiatrist for meds. The Psychiatrist gave none and sent us back to the psychologist. Once there I asked the psychologist why he sent us to the psychiatrist. He said "for marriage counseling." What a waste of time. I said, "Don't you think that is a little late?" Then the psychologist mocked me about my Master's degree and not having a PHD.

Forty plus years and now he cannot talk, cannot do anything to correct the problem. No meds either. But finally, his regular VA doctor gave him mood enhancers which have helped some.

I have been married to my husband for forty-three years. Always hoping things would be better. They only got worst. He sold one of the two houses he had bought for his mother. He bought them before we were married. We lived there for fifteen years. Much too long for a family of five.

He has never bought a house for his own family. He promised a house to us, his family. He actually bought a piece of land to put it on. It was a sham, to keep me from leaving. He even had flowers removed from the second house he bought for his mother and had them planted on the new property. He sold the property. He has never bought a new car for his family. He only bought a new car for himself, a two-seater El Camino. Always a second-hand clunker.

His idea of a vacation is "overnight in a motel". He never strived toward anything. He wanted a business and he got three. But mostly, he just marked time. Tolerating whatever happened. Only existing. Wasting my time.

I realize that some people will think I am a selfish bitch. I suppose I would have to agree to a degree. They do not understand the nature of my life. In this time of free love and women coming into their own. Doing what they want. When they want. I have had none of those experiences. That is the reason I tried to get my girls to understand: getting their education, getting a great job they loved, getting their own money before getting married, and having children. In other words, be happy, be strong, and be empowered before succumbing to dominance by a man. Dominance? Yes. It still exists. Of course, my children are like all children-they didn't listen. But they have success in their own way.

=4=

I can see the potential in everything. I have never been wrong about real estate. But my husband was blind to possibility. He always conferred with my father on any financial idea that I suggested. Purchases I knew would be wealth builders for us. Give us a better life.

I tried many times to get him to invest in property. Houses and commercial property. I suggested a building across from the capital in Tallahassee. For sale $125,000, now worth over a million. A small strip of apartments next to Treasure Island Casino, Las Vegas, Nevada. For sale $125,000, worth millions because Donald Trump's building sits on it now. Spanish house for his family: $35,000 offered to him on a silver platter-now worth nearly one million. Property's which have brought other people wealth. I tried to talk him into anything to bring us out of poverty. But I am female. I am not supposed to see any potential in anything.

He never bought anything for his wife and children. He never invested in 401K, no retirement beyond sheriff department generated, no life insurance to keep his widow comfortable-nothing. He has a twenty-five-thousand-dollar life insurance policy. That is barely enough to bury him. If he dies today-I will get the shaft-just like I have gotten the empty shaft being married to him. It will throw me into poverty worse than I have been living and caring for him.

=5=

Thirty-six years ago, his mother was working as a private care nurse. The patient died and his wife wanted to sell their house. My husband's mother told him to visit the house which is across the street from my parent's house. At his mother's command, we did visit the house. It was a two-story house with a pool. The house was dirty. We needed a house. We were a family of four in a tiny crumpling house. A house he had bought for his mother. A house which she vacated to move to another house he had bought her. We needed a new house. I wanted a new house for our family. Our children. I wanted a house with a pool.

But more importantly, I wanted the Spanish hose across the street from where his mother had worked. I had always lived within twelve blocks of the courthouse, the center of town. As a child I walked past that house to go to town. I had to walk past that house to go to school. That was the only house I had ever really wanted.

My husband and I walked out the back door of the house where his mother had worked. I said, "If you want to buy me a house, I have always wanted the house across the street." To my surprise, with my heart jumping, we walked across the street to the house of my dreams.

A two-story Spanish style house. I never remember the house being any other color than salmon with curved rust colored Spanish roofing tiles. The most prestigious house in town. In the front yard a large old oak tree stretches its' limbs in umbrella fashion. High up in the old oak tree a small palm tree is cradled, embedded in the center of the trunk, where each limb springs outward. The oak tree cradles the palm tree as a mother protecting her young. The palm tree has been cradled there since I was a child.

Mrs. Hendrix opened the door and invited us in to tour the house. I loved it more. The upstairs bathroom needed a little work as did the downstairs laundry. That is all. Mrs. Hendrix said, "This house needs a family. I will sell it to you for thirty-five thousand dollars. I will make it easy for you to buy. You can buy it anyway you like. Rent to own. A loan." She offered the house on a silver platter. I looked at him. "We would decide later." What is to decide? I screamed inside.

Great, we are getting the house I want. He just has to address his mother's suggestion about the dirty house across the street. I waited. At that time, I never spoke up and defended my position on anything (sub-servant). I was still in the oppressed by men mode. I had spoken. I wanted that house for our family. The lady said, "The house needed a family". It had never had children running through it. I wanted it. It was the zenith of success to me. A prestigious house on the main north bound street in Perry. My parents lived in a two-story house on the six hundred blocks. Some people have called their house a "farm house". But that was not the house I wanted. I wanted the Spanish house on the seven-hundred block. It was definitely not a "farmhouse". It screamed success. It screamed home. I screamed inside.

The very next day, when I expected him to come home and say, "We have the Spanish house. We can move in next week."

He said with glee, "Charlie Ware came home from the hospital, drove straight to the house and wrote Grace a check for thirty-five thousand dollars. Charlie could do that; he has plenty of money." The man was relieved he did not have to confront his mother about the house she had suggested.

But me, he ignored. For me, for his family, he did not do anything. The man made no effort whatsoever to buy the Spanish house, I suggested. I wanted. I guess I should have enlisted his mother's help to get what I wanted. I began a spiral of depression. I had no voice. I had no money. I was a female with no job. I was married with two children. I was a female whose opinion did not matter. I had no purchasing power. I was worthless. I then began ridiculing and belittling myself. *Maybe, I did not really want to live near my parents. I did not deserve to have the Spanish house. I was unworthy of such a house. My husband did not care enough for me or his family to buy the house I wanted for our family.* He never noticed. He never cared. It was not his idea. It was not his mother's idea. It was not A MAN'S IDEA.

My father's response to the lady offering the house to us on a silver platter for thirty-five thousand dollars, "I could have bought that house years ago for eighteen thousand dollars." Every time I have ever brought up the Spanish house my father always countered with the same statement. Now my husband can say for the rest of his life, "I could have bought the house for thirty-five thousand dollars on a silver platter." My father went to grave with the same statement. When my husband dies, he can say the same thing,

About fifteen years ago, our oldest daughter and her husband were considering buying a house and the discussion of VA loans and eligibility was discussed in front of me. *Oh boy! Maybe we could get eligibility and apply for what I wanted-although our children are older.* The next day, ON MY HUSBAND'S DRESSER, a paper appeared. The exact paper needed to get a VA loan to buy a house. The VA paper was dated January 1974, a month after his mother died. It had been hidden by him all those years. All those years we could have been raising our three daughters in the Spanish house. I wanted to kill that man-right there on the spot. I screamed and threw a tantrum. I asked that son-of –a-bitch why he did not buy the Spanish house.

"Because we could not afford it." He responded.

I told him, "You're a damn liar. You can tell that lie to anybody else. But I was there when she offered the house on a silver platter."

He laughed. That damn man laughed. I pinned the VA eligibility form over his bedroom door (where he could not get it). Every six months for the last thirty-plus years, when I am in a depressed mood, I blast that damn man for not buying that house or any house for his family. The stroke only delayed my tantrums one year. I don't care that he had a stroke! He is not brain dead. I still blast him. He knows what he did and did not do. He has never made me happy. All he had to do was buy that house. My children are the only thing that made me happy. I have told him I could have gotten my children from a sperm bank. The sperm bank donor would have contributed exactly the same thing to my happiness. Sperm.

He never bought his wife and children a house. He never bought his family anything. But he bought two houses for his mother before we were married. That is what I will put on his tombstone if he dies before me. "Here lies a man who bought two houses for his mother and nothing for his family." I swear it. I have told him I will.

He had worked for Independent Life Insurance with two other guys. All three called Tommy. All three of us got married about the same time. The other two Tommy's built their families new homes. My Tommy did nothing. I do not care or envy what they did for their families. I just care what my husband DID NOT DO FOR HIS FAMILY.

=6=

Financial ideas to make us wealthy-comfortable. I had them, but my ideas have no value. I am female, no penis and balls. Early in our marriage, a female friend, younger than me, was complaining about her husband not letting her buy a car-even though she was working making her own money. She said, without her husband knowing, she had gone to the bank and got a loan to buy the car. I thought about what she had said. I knew that at some point in the future that my husband would say I could not borrow anything. So, I went to a bank president to borrow five hundred dollars to establish my own credit. The bank president insisted he would extend credit to me through my husband. No way. I wanted my own. I did not have a job-I was a homemaker. I did not lie on my loan application. My husband gave me one hundred dollars a month to buy food and such. So, on my loan application I put "self-employed housekeeper", income one hundred dollars per month. My loan was granted. I paid it off.

About six months after paying off the loan, my husband did it.

"You cannot borrow money for anything. You can't do it." He exclaimed in a nonmoving position.

"Yes, I can and I did do it. I have already paid the loan off. I got the loan just because I knew someday you would tell me I couldn't." I don't remember what the discussion was about. But I showed him he did not know everything.

I do remember the very first thing I bought without discussing it with him. I bought a dishwasher from Sears, on credit. When he arrived home and saw the dishwasher, he went ballistic.

"We can't afford that." He exclaimed.

"Yes, we can. I looked at the Sears bill and it was zero." I responded. That took the wind out of his protest. Yeah, for me. I won that round.

I knew that anything that I wanted to do would be met by the same argument as always. We can't afford it. How ya gonna pay for it? And such. So, I decided to do something different-in secret.

I had been forced into taking over my mother's business. Five years of working a money pit business. Five years of hating it. Leaving that business, I tried to help a friend organize her filthy office-business and help her. Help her by using my paralegal knowledge to get her woman owned business certification to do business with the state. I succeeded. She got her certification.

I on the other hand-never ever want to work in filth like that again. They threw their food, coffee and whatever on the floor. I suppose it was supposed to clean its self. I cleaned her office in self-defense. But it was hopeless, even their house looked the same as the business-filthy. I promised myself never to work in such filth again. In secret, I applied for college and was accepted.

When I told my husband and parents about my acceptance, they did exactly what I knew they would do. "How are you going to pay for it?" "How are you going to get there?" Over and over, I responded, "I don't know. But I am going. Things will work out with student loan help and catching a ride with other students. Regardless, I'm going."

On my forty-ninth birthday, I walked into a college auditorium for orientation. My very first time as a college student. My husband drove me to Tallahassee, but he refused to go into the auditorium with me. He sat in the car until I was finished. Five and a half years later, I graduated with two degrees. No major and minor. Two majors. Around 1996 my father realized that I was serious about getting a degree. He bought me a new car. Not a used car. A new car with thirty-two miles on it. My first new car. My father bought it, paid cash. He wanted to make sure I kept going to college. He died two years before I finished. I was proud of myself. But, the Bible says, "Pride cometh before …. something."

Pride cometh before disaster, I presume. As for me that is what it means. I graduated in 2000. I began a job I loved. I was truly just beginning my career. My career. Then my husband put a big fat road block to my future. He had that damn unnecessary surgery which gave him a stroke. Destroyed my career and life.

In this period of history of women, some women will not believe that some women are still oppressed by men. Nor will anyone believe that I have ever been oppressed. Especially after I report that I threw tantrums every six months when I was depressed about my husband not buying his family a house and reliable vehicle. I have put forward a strong bold front since gaining my voice around 1984. I gained my voice, became loud against injustice and laws which are anti-family. I began speaking out at legislative committees until a few laws were changed and new laws added. At all speeches no one knew that I was shaking inside.

I became stronger and stronger. Now I really don't care if anyone agrees with my positions. They are my opinions. I stand behind everyone. I sound off my opinions against the city government, the state government, and the Federal government on a large three-feet by five-feet two-sided sign in my front yard, on the main north bound street, six blocks from the courthouse. Someone asked the mayor to do something about my signs. She told them it was my freedom of speech. I have been putting up signs for fourteen years. I will continue until I can't paint any more. I am loud now. During the last eight years, I have become louder and demanding. I don't know why demanding. Demanding never got me anything from him.

I have been his voice and his demanding champion for recovery. It would have been so easy to do nothing. That would have served him right. I could have done the same as he-nothing. If my husband died tonight, I would be thrown into poverty.

=8=

We have lived in poverty our whole marriage. Just a few dollars above the national low-income level. He worked for the sheriff's department, eight–ten years, until his retirement in 2003. He babysat and transported prisoners. He made almost the same salary as when I married him forty years earlier. He never invested in anything, except the sheriff's state retirement fund and a state funded life insurance policy of five thousand dollars payable at two dollars per month. Two dollars per month! Ridiculous. He spends more than two dollars on cigarettes

He had his paycheck direct deposited into his account, with an automatic saving deduction of twenty-five dollars per week from his paycheck. That is, it. I didn't know what he made. He did not discuss anything with me. I was a female. I never saw his paycheck nor looked at his check book, until after his surgery.

He never listened to any investment ideas I had, because I was female. The exception to investing was for his own desires. He wanted to own his own business. We had been married almost two years when a friend of mine wanted to sell his business. A Hess gas station. He went to the bank. Borrowed the money. He wanted it. He got it.

He had the business four years, during which time the Hess Corporation began forcing all independent dealers out to regain company control of the stations. He spent every morning 'doing PR work' in the coffee room of the Citizen's Bank. Every day he made thousands of dollars deposits. He was depositing hundreds of thousands of dollars every month. But with Hess Corporation forcing independent dealers out of business, his time was up when a check arrived at the bank for more money than was in the checking account at that moment. Overdraft protection was standard practice for this bank. But the bank called him. He requested the bank hold the check for several hours, hours--not days, until he arrived with a deposit to cover the balance of the check. All the years of 'shooting bull crap' in the back room of the bank with the big boys did not pay off. The bank president refused to hold the check another minute. My husband told the bank president, "returning the check would put him out of business". I learned of these events after the fact. It was his business. None of my business.

With the banks help, Hess pushed him out. He immediately bought another business. A gas station. A gas station with a garage. A filthy gas station with a filthy garage. He became a grease monkey. I hated that. It was demeaning to me. It was degrading to me. He bought the business. He did not buy the property. When the gas station property was sold, he purchased an old empty gas station and moved his business across the street. After a few years, he sold the gas station business and became a correction officer. But all these things were things he wanted. Decisions he made. Money, he borrowed to do the things he wanted. He never ever borrowed for the needs of his wife and children.

Part-5

ARE YOU HAPPY?

I was working at my mother's business which I was forced to take over. It was my prison. Every day I wanted to be on the next bus going anywhere. It didn't matter east, west, north or south. It didn't matter I wanted to escape. I hated my life.

Around 1990 I was always working alone, my little Pomeranian dog sitting on her desk nearby, periodically someone would come in. We exchanged needed information and I probably made a sale. But on that day. On that day something different happened. A guy, about two years old than me, came in. I don't remember what he wanted. But I will never forget what he said. He asked me a question. A question no one in my entire life had ever asked me before. He asked me, "Are you happy?"

"Are you happy?" It is a simple sentence. He didn't really care whether I was happy or not. It was a strange question to ask in the context of our transaction. I was so stunned I could not talk. I looked at him. I was silent. I wish I had a photo of how I looked.

"The look on your face says everything. You do not have to answer." He said.

I was not happy then. I am not happy now. I don't expect to be happy in the future.

Recently, my youngest daughter said, "I want to make you happy."

"It is not your job to make me happy." I responded. I think she was stunned by that comment. I let it hang. But later, I explained, "It is her job to make her son happy, not me."

=2=

The experience at Shand's Hospital changed our lives. The person who did not want to be a burden-is a burden. A heavy burden no one should carry. I understand a mother caring for her babies. I understand a mother who wants to make her baby's life better. I understand a mother blaming herself for birth defects or injuries. I understand that. I would, because I am a mother of three girls. I would lay down my life for them.

I understand Terry Schiavo's parent's cry. Terry had fallen into a vegetative state after a cardiac arrest. Her husband wanted to remove Terry's feeding tube so she could die. With no hope of recovery and he said she would not have wanted her life artificially prolonged. Her parents did not want to give up hope.

I understand the hope of a mother whose child is dying of cancer or whatever. I understand the pain when a parent loses a child to suicide. I understand the grief. I heard a male friend say, "No you don't know how I feel." When someone tried to comfort him at his son's viewing. I just gave him a hug and walked away. It was his only biological son. That is a parent's pain.

I would understand if my children had some catastrophic illness and required my help. The Lord gave them to me to love and care for them.

But Lord forgive me. I resent caring for this man, for he gave me nothing but children. I could have gotten my children from a sperm bank and received my children and nothing more. But from a husband and their father, we should have received more than lip-service.

PART-6

EVIDENCE OF FAMILY CRISIS

I wrote the following unpublished papers for a Master's in psychology class. The Family Crisis: Aftermath of Stroke and Stroke Induced Aphasia is a Family Event (2009). The emphasis bears repeating here because it is my story as it is many others. My husband had a stroke and the result beyond paralysis is he has Broca's Aphasia and apraxia. This means he must relearn speech. There is no cognitive disruption.

The Family Crisis: Aftermath of Stroke

Stroke survivors with speech dysfunction and a slow recovery have compounded issues of reduced body mobility, major disruption of family and social norms, as well as depression. But depression is not solitary dilemma for the stroke survivor who must rely on their family caregiver for assistance with daily living activities. Depression bleeds over into the family caregiver, making stroke a family affair. Stroke was identified as a family affair in 1994 (Palmer, et al, 2004). Recognizing that a family is in crisis mode is an essential element under examination by Palmer (2004) who suggests family members must be involved in rehabilitation efforts. Palmer is right that families are in crisis mode during stroke, but their statements are also true of any medical emergency or major illness.

Post-stroke depression in the family caregiver was examined by Tompkins, Schultz, & Rau (1988) to access the adjustments or maladjustments of the family caregiving experience. Although much attention has been paid to the stroke victim and their inpatient care, the outpatient care has been thrust upon the family caregiver. The stroke victim, as well as victims of other major illnesses, which are released to home care, must rely on unequipped family members for daily maintenance needs and support.

Palmer & Glass (2003) examined the families function during stroke recovery and noted that families are left out of the rehabilitative process for the stroke patient. Yet, universally stroke emphasis has been on prevention and not recovery. Stroke can be caused by an unhealthy lifestyle, a closed head injury, an unexpected illness, a fall, or can be the result of surgery gone wrong. Regardless of how the stroke manifested itself, it can do permanent harm to the survivor and their family caregiver. The family caregiver is forced to accept responsibility prematurely of their family member (Palmer, 2004), who has not regained clear cognitive functioning and is subdued by multiple psychotropic drugs. The releasing medical facility ignores the protesting family members request for reduction of drugs and releases patient fully medicated. But this can be also true of other major illnesses. But, unlike other major illness which may not in a recovery mode, but in final stages of death, stroke has no Hospice service for palliative care.

Ketterson, et al. (2000) reported the prestroke and poststroke aphasia clinical assessment measurements do not assess the interaction of stroke aphasic victim's social and family interactions. Although acquired language dysfunction of aphasia is the most disabling and lasting neurocognitive residua of stroke, little is known about the impact communication disruption has between the aphasic and their families. Aphasia is a multimodality communication disorder this disrupts speech in an array of symptoms which vary from patient to patient, therefore assessments and treatments must adapt to accommodate with aggressive therapies.

Stroke Economics and Accessibility

Stroke's physical impairments create economic strain (Palmer, 2003) due to required hospital bed, home modification with wheelchair access ramps, toilet and bathing remodeling, and a surprisingly new perspective toward access to public buildings and the surrounding community environment of our modern world. Although government legislation has addressed the issue of wheelchair accessibility for sidewalks and government buildings, the regulations for private business adapting for handicap facilities are not explicit. The new perspective draws ones attention to how private businesses interpret the regulations of accessibility. Some businesses adapt by adding a handicap bar in toilet areas and a handicap parking sign at the front of the building. But they forget about buildings entry and exit. I found a young severely disabled college student trapped in a college restroom.

Stroke Language Dysfunction

Stroke's speech dysfunction (aphasia) symptoms take many forms based on the location of the injury (Tanner, 2003). Although the Broca's area stroke aphasic victim can talk, the expressive language is disjointed which causes depression, in the victim, as a direct result of not being able to return to prestroke language norms. The contagious effects of frustration and depression spill over into the family caregiver who struggles to understand and adapt to language malfunction. The family of an aphasic individual who refuses to cooperate or makes only minimal effort in their recovery process, frustrates and deepens the family caregiver's depression.

Stroke Daily Functions

Stroke's effects of impaired mobility paralyses create an inability to accomplish daily living necessities and distress within the victim, as well as distress in the family caregiver who must adapt to meet the daily needs of the stroke victim. There is a disruption of social and family norms which are a direct result of stroke.

Family Resilience and Coping Strategies

The disability created by stroke in adults goes beyond four identified causes. Stroke creates a grieving process for the stroke survivor and the family unit. Grief may manifest itself as depression, hopelessness, over-powering anger or no reaction at all. Kubler-Ross (1969) identified five stages of dying in "Death and Dying". Yet, these five stages have also been applied to the grieving process. Dr. Roberta Temes (1991) identified three types of grief behaviors and added them to Kubler-Ross' five stages for stages of grief. Temes stages of grief behavior are (1) numbness stage, (2) disorganization stage and (3) reorganization stage, all of this can be applied to stroke aftermath or any major illness, because the patient is grieving their illness and prestroke abilities.

Cultural Environs

The Terror Management Theory (Pyszxzynski, Greenburg, & Solomon, 1998) identifies culture as a defense mechanism to protect one symbolically from death and grief through religious beliefs. Because individuals and families adapt their beliefs and values around their cultural structures to face the grieving process of a major illness, the coping strategies and family resilience can be an insulation to stroke aftermath.

As a result of the research, I am surprised that the medical and rehabilitative professionals, as well as social workers and psychologist have not and are not on top of this family crisis. Stroke and its aftermath has been an American dilemma for years. Therefore, understanding that the relationship between and focus on family relationships can be a deterrent to family crisis and breakdown in stroke and any major illness should be of immediate concern when an individual enters the medical facility. After, my husband's surgery, the only immediate contact with a hospital social worker was to discuss hotel accommodations. During rehabilitation hospital stay, I made constant request to take my husband off eight psychotropic drugs which were causing him to be agitated. Because of the poor rehabilitative care and inattention, my daughter and I stayed bedside, day and night, for two months. Before release from rehabilitation hospital, no attempt was made to reduce psychotropic drugs, but many attempts were made to get me to sign for additional surgery, which I refused. Before release, the social worker arranged for a speech therapist (who only taught children) and transportation home. Once home, I took control of my husband's recovery and removed all psychotropic drugs and then I was able to access the damage created by an unnecessary and ill-advised surgery which caused his stroke and aphasia.

References:

Kubler-Ross, E., (1969). On death and dying. *Macmillian Publishing Company.*

84

Palmer, S., & Glass, T.A., (2003). Family function and stroke recovery: A review. *Rehabilitation Psychology. 48(4)*, 255-265.

Palmer, S., Glass, T. A., Palmer, J.B., Loo, S., Wegener, S.T., (2004). Crisis intervention with individuals and their families following stroke: A model for psychosocial service during inpatient rehabilitation. *Rehabilitation Psychology. 49(4),* 338-343.

Pyzszynski, T., Greenberg, J., & Solomon, S., (1999). A dual-process model of defense against conscious and unconscious death-related thoughts: An extension of terror management theory. *Psychological Review. 106(4).* 835-845. *American Psychological Association.*

Tanner, D.C., (2003). Eclectic perspectives on the psychology of aphasia. *Journal of Allied Health. 32,* 256.

Temes, R. (1991). Living with an empty chair - a guide through grief. *Irving Publishing.*

Tompkins, C. A., Schultz, R., & Rau, M.T., (1988). Post-stroke depression in primary support persons: Predicting those at risk. *Journal of Consulting and Clinical Psychology. 56,* 502-508.

Stroke Induced Aphasia is a Family Event

ABSTRACT

Stroke is a family crisis which impacts every member of the family unit. The stroke after-effects of limited mobility and speech dysfunction (aphasia) determine the amount of adjustment an individual and a family caregiver must undertake to adapt. The resilience and coping strategies of the individual and the family caregiver determine the successful outcome of post-stroke quality of life. Previous research has indicated that depression is the biggest psychiatric problem following stroke and if a stroke survivor has depression, it is most likely the family caregiver does also. Depression is difficult to identify in stroke induced aphasia victims. However there remains an important gap in the current literature regarding whether aphasia is curable and whether in-home rehabilitation and therapy works. Therefore, the purpose of the proposed study is to identify aphasic stroke patients and their primary family caregiver, before they exit hospital or rehabilitation arenas, to explain the differences in aphasia symptoms, explain signs of depression in both the stroke victim and the family caregiver, provide follow-up in home evaluations for depression and caregiver burnout, and to provide a glimmer of hope for recovery. The traditional methods used to identify depression in stroke victims are useless for aphasic stroke patients who have multimodality systems of aphasia. The findings from this research will help clarify methods of approach to reduce depression in aphasic stroke victim and their family caregiver as well as identify successful recovery methods for aphasia which can improve the quality of life for both stroke victim and family caregiver. This would be an important contribution to the existing literature and would enhance social change initiatives through improved service delivery of information and give hope to families of stroke survivors and reduce stroke aftermath problems which impact quality of life.

Introduction

Aphasia. I had never heard the word in my social sphere. Stroke. I have heard of stroke and the impact it has on the human organism which we inhabit. Yet, I have never experienced stroke or aphasia in my family. But my husband had elective brain surgery which gave him both. All further rehabilitative discussion about stroke and aphasia from doctors have been negative not based on my husband's capabilities, but based on past information about stroke and aphasia (Sisson, 1998).

Aphasia is a speech-language disorder which produces many forms of speech disruption as a direct result of brain injury location. Aphasia for a "motor-mouth" talkative, outgoing individual whose favorite expression was, "I was told I was vaccinated with a Victrola needle." is a life altering event. The strong family roles held by the language impaired stroke survivor no longer exist for him and new instant roles are created for the new family caregiver.

The loss of pre-stroke communication abilities can lead to depression (Siegle & Hasselmo, 2002) and the biggest psychiatric problem following stroke is depression (Sackley, Hoppitt & Cardoso 2005). Therefore, language impaired aphasic stroke victim and their family caregivers face physical, cognitive, and personal adjustment challenges to adapt to loss of speech, loss of mobility, depression, and disruption of quality of life. I know I've been there. After five years, I am still the caregiver of a surgery induced stroke survivor with aphasia. That is my reason for this research.

Problem Statement

Past research has shown that stroke induced aphasia recovery is difficult, time consuming, not optimistic, and will affect an individual's quality of life (Buckwalter, Cusack, Sidles, Wadle, & Beaver, 1989). Advances in geriatrics and in medicine have enabled doctors to prolong the average length of life. But the advancement of age brings increased disabilities associated with aging, the most common of which is communication disorders. Approximately one million Americans are affected with a stroke induced aphasic disorder (Ketterson, Glueckauf, Blonder, Gustofson, Donovan, Rodriquez, Pekich, Ley, & Gonzalez-Rothi, 2008) which is a multimodality communication disorder which produces speech disruption as a direct result of brain injury location (Tanner, 2003). Areas of speech production in the brain are located in (1) Broca's area which produces, when injured, primarily expressive aphasia symptoms, and (2) Wernicke's area which produces, when injured, primarily receptive aphasia symptoms (Pinel, 2002).

Effective communication provides the bases of our everyday lives and is essential for all aspects of medical and rehabilitative care. Aphasic speech dysfunctional symptoms require medical personnel to approach therapy from different positions and with an assumption of effectiveness. Speech-language therapies must be intensive to remediate the deficits (Buckwalter, et al, 1989) caused by stroke induced aphasia, but due to insurance regulations and short lengths of rehabilitation therapy, therapies may be repeated for years with little demonstrable improvements. This compounded with primary physicians who are not aware of any advances of aphasia treatment and who rely on traditional stroke concepts, of no hope for improvement beyond six months (Sisson, 1998), frustrate the aphasic stroke individual and the family caregiver.

The disruption of speech after a stroke prevents immediate diagnosis of depression or immediate diagnosis or prediction of aphasia (Holland & Fridriksson, 2001) and the focus of treatment is on the stroke induced damage to the body organism, not the loss of speech. The loss of communication can lead to depression (Siegle & Hasselmo, 2002) and the biggest psychiatric problem following stroke is depression (Sackley, et al, 2005). But the assessment of a psychological disorder in a stroke induced aphasic patient is difficult because the assessment involves the interaction of cognitive, behavioral, biological, and social interpretations to identify the disorder's mechanisms. The family members may contribute to the assessment by informing medical professionals of the stroke victim's pre-stroke characteristics and quirks, these may not be of much help in the final conclusion if medical professionals refuse to allow the contribution (Holland & Fridriksson, 2001). This rejection of family input into the recovery of their love ones recovery is ethically wrong because the medical professions should do no harm. The family members only want the best medical treatment available and are an intricate part of their family member's recovery. The long–term impact of family caregiving and aphasia recovery with aphasic stroke survivors remains neglected in research.

Although the emotional state of the individual impacted by stroke with aphasic language dysfunction and their family members may be protected by their resilience and coping strategies during a brief recovery, a long recovery period and the realization that the aphasic individual may never return to pre-exiting physical and language norms can be potentially hazardous to a healthy recovery, disruptive to quality of life, and lead to depression for the individual and the family caregiver (Berg, Psych, Palomaki, Lonnqvist, Lehtihalmes, Phil, & Kaste, 2004).

However, an important gap remains in the literature in that we still do not know whether stroke induced aphasia can be reversed with aggressive aphasia therapies such as model-orientated aphasia therapy (MOAT) and constraint-induced aphasia therapy (CIAT) with drug therapy such as memantine. Berthier y Martinez (2007) reports the conventional speech language therapy and several drugs presently used are of little help for those with chronic aphasia. Although Buckwalter (1989) had small results in their research of patients who had been without active speech therapies (an average of 10 years), any communication improvement was a ray of hope for these individuals were significant and improved quality of life. Therefore research to reverse aphasia is paramount to move the stroke aphasic individual and their caregiver toward a semblance of their pre-stroke norms and improve their post-stroke quality of life.

The finding of this paper can help others who face the future of caregiving for an aphasic stroke family member. The cultural interpretation of caregiving for family members varies from country to country, but the effects of stroke and stroke induced speech dysfunction is universal. Any research to improve aphasia speech dysfunction is a ray of hope for these and all families affected by stroke. This paper shall encourage medical professionals to be open to new therapies to address aphasia, and the stress the extreme importance of family caregiver involvement with medical professions to identify pre-stroke characteristics, post-stroke changes, and symptoms of depression in a non-communicative stroke aphasic individual toward effective rehabilitative recovery and improved quality of life.

Integrated Literature Review

Stroke Induced Aphasia and Family Function

Stroke is a family event, not an individual's private escape into themselves. For the individual who experiences stroke and a quick recovery there is a minor inconvenience. But for those individuals who experience a stroke with speech dysfunction and a slow recovery, there is a major disruption of family and social norms. Because stroke is unpredictable it can leave the family vulnerable to depression and stress (Tompkins, Schulz, & Rau, 1988). Warleby, Moller, and Blomstrand (2001) conducted a study of spouses of stroke patients to learn what impact stroke had on the family caregiver. Their findings confirm research of Tompkins, Schulz, and

Rau, although other major illnesses produce stress, little research has been conducted to examine the family reaction in acute stages of stroke. An important issue raised during the study was how stroke patient spouses perceived information received from medical providers and personnel. The spouses reported information received failed to adequately explain the consequences, the severity, the prognosis, and the impact stroke would have on every day events, leaving the family unprepared for the eventual medical care dismissal and aftercare of stroke patient. This failure of adequate information causes the spouses distress and is a possible indicator of future depression due to the large burden caregiving brings to the home.

The burden which stroke induced aphasia brings to the family home is compounded with the loss of speech and creates greater caregiver stress (Han & Haley, 1999). Studies of dementia and Alzheimer's caregiver stress report depression, alcohol use, and susceptibility to disease (Perel, 1998). Caregiver burden and experiences with stroke induced aphasic patients are the same as experiences and burdens of Alzheimer's and dementia caregivers. Yet, we must question why so much interest is focused on Alzheimer's and dementia and whether this is because of decreasing cognitive ability in the patient. Little research interest is paid to stroke victim who has non-decreasing cognitive abilities, but does have behaviors problems similar to Alzheimer's and dementia patients. Research studying stroke induced aphasic survivor's depression and their caregiver's depression, and family function is essentially ignored (Berg, et al., 2005).

Kleiber, Halm, Titler, Montgomery, Johnson, Nicholson, Craft, Buckwalter, and Megivern (1994) suggested a need for interventions for any critical care hospitalization and that includes stroke victims and their families who are in an emotional crisis which needs to be addressed to help the families cope in the hospital and out of the hospital. These interventions may or may not be available in all hospitals.

Palmer and Glass (2003) addressed the issues of family caregiver and family functioning during stroke recovery. Their assertion that stroke is the leading cause of adult disability was confirmed by the American Heart Association (1999). Although Palmer and Glass address the issue of stroke prevention in other countries they are quick to suggest that United States, as well as other developed countries, look more toward rehabilitative efforts post-stoke. But, the rehabilitative efforts of America fall short of being effective in post-stroke aphasia survivors and the issues of home aftercare. The rehabilitative care of stroke individuals and those who have stroke induced speech (aphasia) dysfunction and slow recovery have produced little research to establish the success rate of therapies post-stroke. Buckwalter (1989) also addressed the issue of limited therapies available to aphasic stroke patients, but suggested any therapy even after long breaks is better than none at all. Kotila, Numminen, Waltimo, and Kaste (1998) revealed that post-stroke depression was present three years after stroke and that a small after-discharge rehabilitation program works effectively to prevent post-stroke depression, but few programs are available.

Shockingly, Berg, et al. (2005) asserted caregiver depression was impacted by the severity of stroke and was stronger at the acute stage, but by 18 months post-stroke depression had decreased because of time, which is opposite of studies in Kotila and others. But, Berg redeem themselves by asserting that the assessment of caregivers should be a part of a stroke patient's rehabilitation plan. This is important because the caregiver's medical, social, and emotional needs impact the in-home aftercare of the stroke patient. Depression in the stroke survivor and the burden of caregiving can cause depression and deterioration of health in the caregiver (Kotila, 1998) and lead to cardiovascular disease (Mausbach. Patterson, Rabinowitz, Grant, & Schulz, 2007). Gitlin, Belle, Burgio, Czaja, Mahoney, Gallagher-Thompson, Burns, Hauck, Zhang, Schukz, and Ory, (2003) address caregiver's burdens of individuals suffering dementia. The dementia caregiver's problems are the same as in stroke, yet we find caregiver characteristics may influence caregiver burden and response to any available interventions to alleviate burden and depression. Although some reports have stated coping strategies help the aphasic stroke patient and the caregiver, this may be the same for dementia caregivers also. In 2009, stroke caregivers are still waiting hospital interventions, in-home aftercare therapies, and input into rehabilitation process.

Palmer, Glass, et al (2004) examined crisis intervention for inpatient rehabilitation for stroke victims and their families. But, crisis intervention should also be an outpatient and in home event with stroke victim's families. Shifting medical economic realities of increased cost of hospital stays and decreased coverage of insurance cause stroke patients to be released from medical care prematurely (Ostwald, et al., 2008). The families are unprepared to accept the care giving responsibilities and the over burdening daily needs, of the stroke survivor which can lead to caregiver depression and burn-out. Yet, most intervention studies are with the stroke survivor and conducted without family members who know the individual best (Clark & Smith, 1999). The essential element of rehabilitation for stroke survivors should be the inclusion of the family caregivers (Palmer & Glass et al., 2004) to give insight into the stroke survivor's quirks and mannerisms. To exclude family caregivers is an error of rehabilitation because the family caregiver must address outpatient needs and make adjustments to their environment to accommodate the requirements of any stroke disability.

Stroke Induced Aphasia Family Adjustments

Stroke victims with speech dysfunction have compounded frustration and depression trying to make their caregivers understand their disjointed utterances, personal adjustment, and physical challenges in home environments (Sackley, et al., 2005). Palmer et al (2004) suggested crisis intervention should be undertaken for stroke in-patients and their families because depression is a major issue in both the survivor and the family caregivers. Depression in family members was examined by Tompkins, Schultz, & Rau (1988) who asserted the risks of post stroke depression in families may affect the quality of life for the survivor and their caregivers, also, depression in the caregiver could lead to caregiver neglect of stroke victim.

The risk for caregiver depression can't be drawn merely from inpatient stroke victim's deficits and future needs, because inpatient events can't predict in home environmental and physical adjustments, family norms or social functioning of a non-communicating individual. Berg et al (2005) asserts stroke patients depression is not as common as the caregivers depression (23% to 29%) and the depression is seen earlier in the caregiver. Even though Berg did not address caregiver exhaustion as a factor influencing depression in their study, they did report that exhaustion caused by caregiving burden, may be a part of depression for the caregiver.

The shock and sudden onset of stroke impacts the family lifestyle and can be psychologically, emotionally, and physically draining on both the caregiver and stroke victim (Perrin, et al., 2008). The devastating psychological impact of stroke with aphasia require significant coping adjustments for the survivor and the caregiver. The coping and reactive nature of stroke survivor and family members receive little attention by the medical profession because they are attending to the attack on the human organism. Medical professionals do not pay attention to stroke survivor's and family member's emotional issues although the symptoms are known to influence the neurological outcome of the stroke patient recovery (Fure, Wyller, Engedal, & Thommesson, 2006). Early identification of issues beyond the physical symptoms of stroke is an important aspect of recovery that medical professionals must under-take to prevent post-stroke depression, emotional stress, and suffering for years post-stroke for the survivor and family caregiver (Kleiber, et al., 1994). The emotional turmoil created by a critical care hospitalization must be addressed through accurate information and coping interventions to assist family members to understand their reactions and adapt for the successful medical dismissal of the stroke survivor. But, few interventions are available to the survivor and their family.

Non-communicating aphasic stroke survivor's emotional crisis is impossible to diagnosis immediately post-stroke, but the reactive emotional trauma of the family are not. Therefore it is imperative that medical professionals involve family members in the rehabilitative process before medical dismissal. Taking a fully medicated non-communicating aphasic stroke patient home is a great shock to family members and requires hurried environmental changes and restructuring of daily life to surround a hospital bed. Further examination must be undertaken to provide insight into the psychosocial impact the act of caregiving places on the caregiver. With stroke caregiver's depression estimated at 40-50% in 1990's, a review of the family systems approach to stroke recovery is important because of increased family mobility and social lifestyles which could produce greater depression percentages (Palmer, et al., 2003).

A call for further research on the impact of stroke on family support systems, psychosocial adjustments, and crisis interventions are an important step toward helping stroke survivors and their families. The impact of long-term family caregiving complexities and the caregiving experience of an aphasic stroke survivor have not been evaluated. An essential element of aphasic stroke survivor follow-up therapies is speech therapy, but little research addresses the importance of family caregiver to motivation and recovery of speech. The medical professional ignoring the caregiver input in rehabilitation efforts is compounded by the exclusion of family caregiver in the speech rehabilitation. When aphasic stroke survivor needs sentence structure in speech rehabilitation, he is met with single word formations for years. The formation of single words are harder to formulate than sentences, because searching for single word is frustrating. This leads to greater depression and rejection of therapy.

Resources Synthesis and Integration

Family Adjustments to Stroke and Recovery

Brain or nervous system injury can result in one or a combination of communication disorders, two of which are called aphasia. However with stroke you may have a combination of communication disorders and a single or multiple body part immobilizations. Stroke is a schematic attack on the brain's nervous system and is the leading cause of adult disability in the United States with approximately three million people living with stroke related issues (Palmer & Thomas, 2003). A stroke is instant, no individual or family member is prepared for the event. It happens. Can we be prepared? No. The individual as well as the family must recover from the shock of stroke and its' after effects to address how to adapt to loss of communication and immobilization.

Tompkins, Schulz, & Rau (1988), Holland & Fridriksson (2001), Palmer & Glass (2003), and Palmer, et al (2004) all contribute similar positions on stroke induced aphasic survivors and their caregivers. The importance of family function and the psychosocial wellbeing of both the stroke survivor and the family caregiver are essential elements of any recovery process. But, Palmer & Glass (2003) and Palmer et al. (2004) stress the importance of family interventions in and out of medical and therapy events. The interventions inform families of coping strategies and necessary adjustments required of the survivor and the caregiver. The adjustments of life norms and social restricting of the family unit is also reported by Tompkins, Schulz & Rau (1998) to develop a semblance of pre-existing norms. The struggle of the family unit adjusting to the trauma before it throws family out of whack and needs adjustments to adapt to the new future plans of the family (Holland & Fridriksson, 2001). The conjoining consensus of all research brings our attention to the importance of family members and family caregivers in the need of crisis interventions in hospital settings and rehabilitative recommendations and assistance. The exclusion thereof creates greater stress in the survivor and the family caregiver.

Stroke and Dissonance

Stroke is the leading cause of communication disorders which impairs the adult's ability to use language as they are accustomed (Holland & Fridriksson, 2001). The patient experiences cognitive dissonance in that there is no cognitive disability, but the language abilities and behavior suggest that there is. The dissonance of language impaired aphasic stroke victim trying to return to pre-existing abilities impacts the family caregiver trying to understand and meet the required maintenance needs of the victim. Although the family caregiver has no cognitive disability there is a dissonance of conflicting external servitude (good behavior) behavior which is necessary care for the aphasic stroke victim and the internal anger (bad behavior) toward the aphasic stroke victim for putting the caregiver in the servitude position. For the aphasic stroke victim there is a dissonance between thoughts and words. For the family caregiver there is dissonance between responsibility and rejection of responsibility. How we assess the meaning and significance of our behavior creates our own dissonance (Stone, 2000, Poulshock & Demling, 1984). Therefore, the family caregiver's issues of environmental self standards of normal expected behavior and the unexpected behavioral reaction to imposed role of caregiver causes dissonance and adjustment problems (Tompkins, et al 1998). Thus social and emotional support of family member's within the aphasic stroke victim's sphere is important to the victim's recovery and to reduce the caregiver's guilt for having responsibility rejection issues.

Family Self Reliance

Cost controls and insurance issues force patients in and out of rehabilitative care without restoration of self-care, psychological equilibrium, and social functioning (Palmer, et al 2004). This throws the patient and their family, who have not adapted to the new role of victims of stroke, into turmoil (Fure, 2006). The psychosocial transitions required of the stroke victim and their family caregiver create a reconstruction of whole family functioning to accommodate both temporary and permanent changes (Palmer & Glass, 2003). Family resilience and adaptive capacities are under attack when it is presented with aphasic stroke adjustments. Aphasic stroke presents challenges for the victim's physical and cognitive capabilities, to social interactions, family relations, and prevents an individual's independent return to the community. As a result some are calling stroke a "family dilemma" and suggest closer examination must be focused on the primary family caregiver (Palmer, et al. 2004) from a family systems perspective. Stroke rehabilitation is not only about the individual's recovery; it is a collaborative process through which the whole family must proceed, especially the primary family caregiver. The primary family caregiver who carries the caregiver burden and majority of caregiver responsibilities are at risk for caregiver burn-out, and experience a decline in their own health and other psychosocial problems including depression.

Family Depression

Depression in stroke survivors and family caregivers is common (Berg, 2004). Although depression is the biggest psychiatric complication following stroke, evaluation of depression is impossible in aphasic stroke patients. The assessment of depression requires the interaction of cognitive, behavioral, and social interactions to identify the disorder's mechanisms which are disabled by aphasic stroke affects. Declaring depression and family function are closely related, Palmer, et al (2004) posit that stroke is a family psychosocial crisis, springing from the emotional impact of stroke and the unpreparedness of families to accept the burden of caregiving and lack of support. All of which can contribute to depression in stroke survivor and family caregiver. Tompkins et al (1988) suggest the need for evaluating family caregivers who may be at risk of psychosocial problems in the aftermath of stroke. Whether family caregivers develop depression cannot be based on the predictions of the stroke survivor's stroke-related deficits. Some form of depression is inevitable in both stroke survivor and their family caregiver. Although the emotional ties may be strong, the failure of stroke survivor to return to pre-existing norms and the family caregiver's burden of caregiver responsibilities, place both on a one-way track to destruction, if no outside intervention is available to both. In small towns where no counseling intervention services and homebound assist services are not available, the possibility of increased emotional turmoil and caregiver burn-out is waiting for the caregiver.

Life Satisfaction and Quality of Life

Stroke disrupts family life norms and family's perception of life (Segal & Schall, 1996). Segal and Schall explored the stroke survivor's and their caregiver's quality of life in terms of life satisfaction and it's correlation to burden of disability and handicap of survivor. Basing their hypothesis of stroke on the definitions of the World Health Organization's 1980 definitions of disability and handicap. Therein disability was one or more psychological, anatomical or function impairment and handicap was the total sum effect of disability of social norms in the environment and performance thereof. Segal and Schall found a demonstrable difference in the interpretation of disability and handicap for the stroke survivor. Life satisfaction for the survivor was due to limits created by disability. But, the caregiver's perception of life satisfaction was directly related to the amount of physical disability and the burden of care it created.

Predicting emotional problems and depression of stroke survivor's spouse or caregiver has been the subject of many studies. But the predictions of these issues based on the stroke survivor's deficits in-hospital stay is not reliable and in-hospital rehabilitation may not carry over to the home environment (Tompkins,1988). Also, there are no follow-up studies of the effectiveness of in-hospital rehabilitation continuing to the home environment. Visser-Meily, Post, Schepers, and Lindeman (2005) examined spouse's quality of life and life satisfaction one year post-stroke to conclude that caregivers must be identified at the beginning of the stroke rehabilitation process to deter depression and impairment of life satisfaction and quality of life.

Stroke Aftercare

A Stroke survivor's identity is important in recovery (Palmer & Glass, 2003) and the loss created by stroke alters their perception of life after stroke capabilities. There are a small number of intervention programs in hospital settings, but they are non-existent in the home and small towns. Where aphasic stroke patient interventions are available in hospital settings, they are conducted without family members' participation. These interventions are used to address the natural coping strategies of the survivor and would help family members who may become the primary caregiver in the home. The psychosocial intervention is important for adapting to stroke after effects for both the stroke survivor and the family caregiver. Palmer, et al (2004) suggest a combination of cognitive behavioral techniques, psychosocial and crisis interventions are important for the survivor.

Tompkins, Schulz, and Rau (1988) brought attention to the family in predicting depression in family caregivers. Although there is literature available about prediction of depression, health, and other issues impacting the family caregiver and the stroke survivor there is little research about in home aftercare programs nor are they available. In follow-up speech therapies, the stroke survivor must be transported to a facility and the traditional speech therapy methods used are with the exclusion of the family caregiver.

Family members face an emotional crisis in stroke and are in a crisis mode following the stroke of their loved ones. Therefore the mental and physical health of the family caregiver must remain intact to ensure the aphasic stroke survivor can remain at home and not require institutionalization (Watson, Modeste, Catolico, & Crouch, 1998). Research of the negative effect the burden of caregiving creates has led to development of tests to alleviate burdens and depression for dementia patient caregivers (Gitlin, et al, 2003), but these test are not available to the aphasic stroke patient caregivers. Dementia patients have behavioral problems as well as emotional and cognitive issues. Yet, no research is available which documents behavioral the problems of the stroke patient. But aphasic stroke patients have behavioral problems which are ignored by the medical professions. This paper is directed toward research of Broca's aphasia. The Broca's aphasia stroke survivor has no problems with cognitive function and is fully aware of his temper tantrums and demands imposed on the family caregiver. From a personal point of view, the caregiver's life is in jeopardy when a fully cognitive Broca's aphasic stroke survivor throws a temper tantrum and grabs the steering wheel of a vehicle moving at speed of eighty in heavy traffic. Counseling interventions, in hospital and in home, are essential and appropriate for this aphasic and needed for the caregiver's sanity and safety.

CRITICAL ANALYSIS

Stroke Induced Aphasia is a Family Event

There have been many efforts to analyze the impact of stroke induced aphasia on patients. But, aphasia symptoms vary from patient to patient making it a difficult course of diagnosis and treatment.   Stroke survivors with speech dysfunction and a slow recovery have compounded issues of reduced body mobility, major disruption of family and social norms, as well as depression grieving the loss of pre-existing abilities and varying degrees of speech loss. But depression is not solitary dilemma for the stroke survivor who must rely on their family caregiver for post-stroke assistance with daily living activities. Depression can also affect the family caregiver, making stroke a family affair. Stroke was identified as a family affair in 1994 (Palmer, et al 2003). Recognizing that a family is in emotional (Kleiber, et al., 1994) and crisis mode, by the sudden onset of stroke, is an essential element under examination by Palmer et al. who suggest family members must be involved in recovery rehabilitation step. Palmer et al. is right that families are in crisis mode during stroke, but their statements are also true of any medical emergency or major illness. But in stroke induced aphasia the issues of little or no method of communication, limited mobility, disruption of normal family life and social norms impact quality of life for the survivor and the family members. Yet little research has been conducted with family caregivers or the residual effectiveness of rehabilitation efforts in the home environment. In the research available there is debate whether depression in stroke induced aphasic patient has a bearing on the post-stroke depression and physical health of caregivers (Berg, et al 2006). But looking at dementia research, dementia caregiver stress has produced increased depression, alcohol use, and a susceptibility to disease (Perel, 1998). Stroke creates all of these and creates cardiovascular disease within seven years post stroke (Visser-Meily,

Post, Schepers, & Linderman, 2005).

Palmer and Glass (2003) direct our attention to the strain on existing family relationships to adapt to the temporary and permanent changes stroke creates, but researchers focus on the individual stroke patient rather than the family as a whole. Post-stroke depression of family caregivers was examined by Tompkins, Schultz, & Rau (1988) to access the adjustments or maladjustments of the family caregiving experience. Although much attention has been paid to the stroke victim and their inpatient care, the outpatient care has been thrust upon the unprepared family caregiver. Greater concern was focused on the issue of quality of life and the potential for depression of the caregiver spouse, but predicting post-stroke depression in the care giving spouse cannot be predicted from the stoke patient's deficits because coping strategies must be considered.

Family Resilience and Coping Strategies

The disability created by stroke in adults goes beyond obvious identified causes. Stroke creates a grieving process for the stroke survivor and the family unit. Grief may manifest itself as depression, hopelessness, over-powering anger or no reaction at all. Kubler-Ross (1969) indentified five stages of dying in "Death and Dying". Yet, these five stages have also been applied to the grieving process. Dr. Roberta Temes (1991) identified three types of grief behaviors and added them to Kubler-Ross' five stages for stages of grief. Temes stages of grief behaviors are (1) numbness stage, (2) disorganization stage and (3) reorganization stage, all of this can be applied to stroke aftermath or any major illness, because the patient is grieving their illness and pre-stroke abilities.

Stroke Aftermath

Palmer & Glass (2003) examined the families' function during stroke recovery and noted that families are left out of the rehabilitative process for the stroke patient. Yet, universally stroke emphasis has been on prevention and not recovery. Stroke can be caused by an unhealthy lifestyle, a closed head injury, an unexpected illness, a fall, or can be the result of surgery gone wrong. Regardless of how the stroke manifested itself, it can do permanent harm to the survivor and their family caregiver. The family caregiver is forced to accept responsibility prematurely of their family member (Palmer, 2004), who may not have regained clear cognitive functioning and is subdued by multiple psychotropic drugs. In this caregiver experience the aphasic stroke survivor was released fully medicated with eighteen psychotropic drugs. The releasing medical facility ignored the protesting family members request for reduction of drugs and released patient fully medicated. But, this could also true of other major illnesses.

Ketterson, et al. (2000) reported pre-stroke and post-stroke aphasia clinical assessment measurements do not assess the interaction of stroke aphasic victim's social and family interactions which is important for a full appraisal of future adjustments. Although acquired language dysfunction of aphasia is the most disabling and lasting neurocognitive residua of stroke, little is known about the impact communication disruption has between the aphasic and their families. Aphasia is a multimodality communication disorder which disrupts speech in an array of symptoms which vary from patient to patient, therefore assessments and treatments must adapt to accommodate with aggressive therapies.

Stroke Economics and Accessibility

Stroke's physical impairments create economic strain (Palmer, 2003) due to required hospital bed, home modification with wheelchair access ramps, toilet and bathing remodeling, and a surprisingly new perspective toward access to public buildings and the surrounding community environment of our modern world. Although government legislation has addressed the issue of wheelchair accessibility for sidewalks and government buildings, the regulations for private business adapting for handicap facilities are not explicit. The new perspective draws ones attention to how private businesses interpret the regulations of accessibility. Some businesses adapt by adding a handicap bar in the toilet areas and a handicap parking sign at the front of the building. But, they forget about buildings entry and exit doors.

The stroke victim, as well as victims of other major illnesses, who are released to home care must rely on unequipped family members for daily maintenance needs and support. But unlike other major illnesses, the primary difference between a home bound non-terminally ill stroke patient and a home bound terminally ill patient is in home support received from hospice assistance. If the patient is over fifty they may receive senior services for needed bathing assistance. But this type of services is not always available in small towns.

Stroke Language Dysfunction

Stroke's speech dysfunction (aphasia) symptoms take many forms based on the location of the injury (Tanner, 2003). Broca's aphasic individual remains cognitive but has difficulty expressing himself in pre-existing norms. Although, the Broca's area stroke aphasic victim can talk, the expressive language is disjointed which causes depression, in the victim, as a direct result of not being able to return to pre-stroke language norms. The stroke survivor's contagious effects of frustration and depression impacts the family caregiver who struggles to understand and adapt to language malfunction and daily living needs of stroke survivor.

Stroke Daily Functions

Stroke's effects of impaired mobility paralyses creates an inability to accomplish daily living necessities and distress within the victim, as well as distress in the family caregiver who must adapt to meet the daily needs of the stroke victim. The Broca's aphasic stroke survivor can be demanding and self-centered without consideration of the family caregiver. Speech is slow and writing is haltingly accomplished, but the message is clear and demanding. There is a complete family disruption of social and family norms.

Dooley, Shaffer, Lance, Williamson (2007) suggest informal care by family caregivers can be a better fit for families to prevent institutionalization. But there is no measurement or consensus how to measure this aftercare for stroke, or any other illness or age. Due to the aging population , with an estimated 39 million American families potentially providing aftercare, and the increased potential for family home care there is concern that abuse may become a problem. Abuse of the ill or the aged may be avoided by counseling and interventions suggested by Palmer & Glass (2003) and Palmer et al. (2004) to help families cope and avoid depression which could lead to abuse.

Cultural Environs

The Terror Management Theory (Pyszxzynski, Greenburg, & Solomon, 1998) identifies culture as a defense mechanism to protect one symbolically from death and grief through religious beliefs. Because individuals and families adapt their beliefs and values around their cultural structures to face the grieving process of a major illness, the coping strategies and family resilience can be an insulation to stroke aftermath and strive for self-preservation. The counseling and interventions suggested by Palmer & Glass (2003) and Palmer et al. (2004) can also overcome the fears as a precaution against family failure to adapt or cope to stress.

Stroke Aftercare

Although hospice is available for end-of-life necessities of the terminal ill patients, there is no such services for stroke aphasic or other illnesses which affect continuing of life issues. The aftermath of stroke creates a grieving process for the stroke aphasic individual and the family caregiver. Their grief began at the instant of stroke, although different in issue grieved, they both grieve for loss of family norms and social norms. It has been reported that after stroke life expectancy is seven years in a normal stroke induction. Yet, some experience stroke because of botched surgery, therefore to say life expectancy is only seven years may not apply to these individuals. If we interpret the life expectancy to overall stroke individuals, families must prepare for anticipated death which creates a new area for increased depression, stress, and grief of impending loss.

As a result of the research, medical and rehabilitative professionals, as well as social workers and psychologist have not and are not on top of this family crisis. Stroke and its aftermath has been an American dilemma for years. Therefore understanding that the relationship between and focus on family relationships can be a deterrent to family crisis and breakdown in stroke and any major illness should be of immediate concern when an individual enters the medical facility.

Social Significance of the Study

Stroke has no reverence for age, skin color, cultural traditions, or global location, it takes its' toll at any moment of time without warning. The topic of long-term family caregiving, the family caregiver, and the stroke induced aphasia survivor are of social significant because stroke with communication dysfunction is common (Buckwalter et al. 1989). The projected number of aging population has increased with the advancement of modern medicine (Ketterson et al. 2008). Therefore consideration of long-term care must become a significant part of our future family plans. The family caregiver will become a valuable asset to every family and bring different insight to the recovery process than a paid non-family caregiver.

As a family caregiver I am my husband's lifeline against institutionalization. What social significance does this make in the over-all picture of social significance of world view?

Everyone can, in an instance, become a caregiver just like me. Stroke has no reverence for age, skin color, cultural traditions, or global location, it takes its' toll at any moment of time without warning. I, the caregiver have my frame of reference and expertise of the events of stroke induced aphasia survivor with medical facilities, with medical professionals, with speech and physical therapist. My experience with each of these professionals has been met by a negative projection of no hope for any recovery. What is there for mankind if it is without hope?

Proposed Resolution

Recommendations for the Future

Stroke and stroke induced aphasia creates problems for the family which may or may not be overcome by counseling interventions at hospital and rehabilitative level of care. The identified problem of stroke with aphasia is the medical profession's neglect of event aftermath and aftercare. Both aftermath and aftercare require some participation by the stroke survivor and family members, especially the family caregiver.

The medical profession's attention is directed to stabilization of the human organism during hospital stay and dismissal to rehabilitation. The hospital social worker provides, to the family members, information about rehabilitation and rehabilitation dismissal and where to acquire hospital bed and other items needed for the survivor's return home. Little or no attention is given to the impact stroke has on the family unit; nor is any attention directed toward aftercare and the burden of aftercare on potential family caregiver, unless the person is terminally ill. But the stroke survivor may not be terminally ill and no in home service is available to those who are not terminal. Hospice services are available only to the terminally ill not permanently disabled. As a result of stroke, the primary objective of medical establishments is to focus on stabilization of the human organism, not aftermath or aftercare.

The goal of developing a resolution to the professional neglect of aftermath and aftercare is an established plan of action to address the emotional crisis and turmoil of the stroke family and the stroke survivor. A plan which formulates steps toward healthy coping strategies for the stroke survivor and the stroke family members, pre-release of medical and rehabilitative establishments.

Possible solutions:

1. Develop list of possible aftermath and aftercare scenarios of stroke and stroke induced aphasia for family members. The aftermath and aftercare scenarios can prepare families, before patient is released from medical care, for possible outcomes of stroke. The advantage of presenting families with written scenarios is the family is in shock and crisis mode and may not absorb any information beyond "the patient is alive, but not with pre-stroke capabilities of language and mobility." The disadvantage to written scenarios is the family members are in a state of emotional turmoil and shock responding to stroke aphasic event. They become frighten by prospect of post stroke-aphasic outcome and become unable to function and develop depression. The cost of seeking medical care for the family caregiver increases. The cost the medical establishments is minimal, and a positive social relationship toward overall community health is maintained. The challenge is to convince medical establishments of the benefits of their clients and community health.

2) The medical, psychological, and social worker organizations must develop an in hospital counseling intervention service for family members to prepare them for possible post stroke events and post-stroke care needs. The advantages of family in hospital counseling helps families reduce possibility of depression, increase coping strategies to handle stroke aphasic aftermath and aftercare needs and prevents decreased quality of life. The cost are minimal and the advantages are a preventive health deterioration measure in family caregivers. The challenge is convincing professionals this is a needed service.

3) Medical professions must recognize the need to develop programs to assist family caregivers to maintain aftercare quality of life. Provide a list of available aftercare services to

meet the needs of homebound care (bathing, meals, lifting, transporting) and available caregiver respite services. The disadvantages are cost of follow-up care may not be covered by insurance or unaffordable. Housing modification may be impossible for families who do not own their own home to adapt to post-stroke immobility. The advantage of these programs is to assist family caregivers is a preventive measure to ensure caregiver health, reduce or prevent caregiver burnout which in turn helps in stroke survivor recovery. The disadvantage is the limited availability of services locally, nationally, and globally. The challenge is convincing professionals of necessity of services.

4) Educate physicians, social workers, and other medical personnel about new treatments of aphasia to give hope to the stroke family and to treat family members and family caregivers as individuals who have knowledge of the characteristics and quirks of the patient. Require physicians, social workers, and other medical personnel to treat family caregivers with respect. The advantage is improved medical care. Reduces families feelings of inadequateness and emotional distress in medical setting. The disadvantage is professional rejection of family members contribution to the recovery of stroke-aphasic patient, although research has shown that family members contribute to the recovery process but have been ignored as an essential element of recovery.

5) Educate physicians by dispensing simple abstracts of new research which addresses issues of recovery for individual major illness or aftermath, specifically stroke induced aphasia. Educate medical professionals that new therapies are available for aphasia treatments and aphasia may also be of an organic nature, wherein drugs combined with aggressive speech therapy can produce recovery results. Educate medical professionals that aphasia takes many forms and produce different symptoms and each require different approaches to therapy. The advantage of this education would be more family friendly medical environment and improve family confidence in medical professionals. The disadvantage and challenge of implementing

this is the arrogance of some medical professionals who reject anything new or family members input into the direction of patient care.

Conclusion

Stroke induced aphasia, particularly Broca's aphasia is a frustrating, timing consuming and slow recovery, medical condition that any individual can acquire. Unlike other aphasia symptoms which can also be frustrating and time consuming, Broca's aphasics can have a recovery. A recovery of language even after 11 years of struggle is possible (Bertheir y Martinez, G., 2007). This is because there is confusion and debate as to whether Broca's aphasia is a result of the brain organism's physical damage or a result of a chemical reaction to brain injury. Research trials of constraint speech therapy combined with drugs typically used in dementia and Alzheimer patients have produced surprising treatment results. These research treatments are a glimmer of hope for those families who have received nothing but negative information from their stroke surviving family member's medical professionals and speech therapist. Hope is always a light which the family caregiver and the stroke survivor must cling to in order to avoid depression and inspire coping strategies. The failure of medical professionals and speech therapist to stay informed of new research and treatment is unprofessional and destructive to the stroke survivor and family caregiver. The findings of this study can be a catalyst for social change within the medical community to improve healthcare across the globe.

My experience as the only caregiver of a stroke survivor with Broca's aphasia has been the most frustrating, depressing, and emotionally draining experience of my life and I wish it on no one. Although I know that research is out there to treat my husband, I have none near our home and none which I can afford. We have no insurance because I had to give up my job to care for him. His medical issues are addressed by the Veteran's Administration's hospital and outpatient clinics. What is really annoying is the research discovered in this capstone project has shown that the Veteran's Administration has backed many trials for stroke, dementia, and Alzheimer's disease, but the medical staff are unaware of these trials, nor do they provide the drugs used in the trials. So where does that leave us?

References:

American Heart Association (1999). Heart and Stroke Statistical Update. Dallas, Tex: American Heart Association, 2000.

Barthel, G., Meinzer, M., Djundja, D., Rockstroh, B. (2008). Intensive language therapy in chronic aphasia: Which aspects contribute most? *Aphasiology, 22(4)*, 408-421.

Berg, A., Palomaki, H., Lonnqvist, J., Lehtihalmes, M., & Kaste, M. (2005). Depression among caregivers of stroke survivors. *Stroke: Journal of the American Heart Association, 3*, 639-643.

Bertheir y Martinez, G. (2007). Memantine and intensive speech-language therapy in aphasia.

Buckwalter, K.C., Cusack, D., Sidles, E., Wadle, K., Beaver, M. (1989). Increasing communication ability in aphasic/dysarthric patients. *Western Journal of Nursing Research. 11(6)*, 736-747. Sage Publications.

Clark, M.S., & Smith, D.S. (1999). Psychological correlates of outcomes following rehabilitation from stroke. *Clinical Rehabilitation, 13(2)*, 129-140.

Dooley, W.K., Shaffer, D.R., Lance, C. E., & Williamson, G. (2007). Informal care can be better than adequate: Development and evaluation of the exemplary care scale. *Rehabilitation Psychology, 52(4)*, 359-369.

Gitlin, L.N., Belle, S.H., Burgio, L.D., Czaja, S.J., Mahoney, D., Gallagher-Thompson, D., Burns, R., Hauck,W.W., Zhang, S., Schukz, R., and Ory, M.C. (2003). Effect of multicomponent interventions on caregiver burden and depression: The reach multisite intiative at 5-month flow-up. *Psychology and Aging, 18 (3)*.361-374.

Forsberg-Warleby, G., Moller, A., Blomstrand, C. (2001). Spouses of first-ever stroke patients:

Psychological well-being in the first phase of after stroke. *Stroke: Journal of The American Heart Association. 32*, 1646-1651.

Fure, B., Wyller, T.B., Engeedal, K., Thommessen, B. (2006). Emotional symptoms in acute ischemic stroke. *International Journal of Geriatric Psychiatry*, 21, 82-387.

Han, B., & Hanley, W.E. (1999, July). Family caregiving for patients with stroke: Review and Analysis. *Stroke. 30*, 1478-1485.

Holland, A. & Fridriksson, J. (2001). Aphasia management during the early phases of recovery following stroke. *American Journal of Speech-Language Pathology, 10*, 19-28.

Ketterson, T.U., Glueckauf, R.I., Blonder, L.X., Gustofson, D.J., Donovan, N.J., Rodriquez, A.D., Pekich. D., Ley, C., Gonzalez-Rothi, L.J. (2008). Reliability and validity of the functional outcome questionnaire for aphasia (FOQ-A).

Kleiber, C., Halm, M., Titler, M., Montgomery, L.A., Johnson, S.K., Nicholson, A., Craft, M., Buckwalter, & Megivern, K. (1994). Emotional responses of family members during a critical care hospitalization. *American Journal of Critical Care, 3(1)*, 70-76.

Kotila, M., Numminen, H., Waltimo, O., Kaste, M. (1998). Depression after stroke: Results of the Finnstroke study. *Stroke: Journal of the American Heart Association, 29*, 368-372.

Kubler-Ross, E. (1969). On Death and Dying.

Mausbach, B.T., Patterson, T.L., Rabinowirz, G., Grant, I., & Schulz, R. (2005). Depression and Distress predict time to cardiovascular disease in dementia caregivers. *Health Psychology, 26(5)*, 539-544.

Ostwald, S.K., Davis, S., Hersch, G., Kelley, C., Godwin, K.M. (2008). Evidenced-based educational guidelines for stroke survivors after discharge home. *Journal of Neuroscience Nursing, 40(3)*, 173-191.

Palmer, S., Thomas, A.G. (2003). Family function and stroke recovery: A review. *Rehabilitative Psychology, 48*, 255-265.

Perel, V.D. (1998). Psychosocial impact of alzheimer disease. *Journal of the American Medical Association, 279(13),* 1038-1039.

Perrin, P.B., Heesacker, M., Studham, B.S., Rittman, M., Gonzalez-Rothi, L.J. (2008). Structural equation modeling of the relationship between caregiver psychosocial variables and functioning of individuals with stroke. *Rehabilitation Psychology, 53(1),* 54-62.

Pinel, John P.J. (2002). *Biopsychology, 5th.* 428. Allyn and Bacon. Boston, MA.

Poulshock, & Demling, 1984).

Sackley, C.M., Hoppitt, T.J., Cardoso, K. (2005). An investigation into the utility of the stroke aphasic depression questionnanaire (SADQ) in care home settings. *Clinical Rehabilitation, 20,* 598-602.

Segal, M.E., & Schall, R.R., (1996). Life satisfaction and caregiving stress for individuals with stroke and their primary caregivers. *Rehabilitation Psychology, 41(4),*303-.

Siegle, G.J., Hasselmo, M.E. (2002). Using connectionist models to guide assessment of psychological disorder. *Psychological Assessment, 14(3),* 263-278.

Sisson, R.A. (1998). Life after stroke: Living with change. *Rehabilitation Nursing. 28,* 198-203.

Stone. J., Cooper, J. (2000). A self-standards model of cognitive dissonance. *Journal of Allied Health, 32,* 256.

Tanner, D.C. (2003). Eclectic perspectives on the psychology of aphasia. *Journal of Allied Health, 32,* 256.

Tompkins, C.A., Schulz, R., & Rau, M.T. (1988). Post-stroke depression in primary support persons: Predicting those at risk. *Journal of Consulting and Clinical Psychology, 56,* 502-508.

Visser-Meo;y, A., Post, M., Schepers, V., & Lindeman, E., (2005). Spouses' quality of life 1 year after stroke: Prediction at the start of clinical rehabilitation. *Cerebrovascular*

Diseases 20. 443-448.

Watson, R., Modeste, N.N., Catolico, O., & Crouch, M., (1998). The relationship between

caregiver burden and self-care deficts in rehabilation patients. *Rehabilitation Nursing 23,*

258-262.

Warleby, Moller, & Blomstrand (2001)

World Health Organization. (1980). International classifications of impairments. disabilities, and

handicaps. Geneva: WHO.

Reference: Aphasia. Retrieved July 7, 2011 from MedicineNet, Inc.

http://www.medicinenet.com/aphasia/page2.htm.

Apraxia. Retrieved July 12, 2011. National Institute of Deafness and other communication

disorders. www.nidcd.nih.gov/directory

PART 7

I HATE CAREGIVING

The above referenced material was last reviewed in 2010, but that is not the end of the story. We returned to Perry and my husband continued to gain weight, it became harder to get him in and out of the house. The VA gave him a powerchair and suggested a Handicap ramp. The ramp was installed and I discovered the builder did not secure two aluminum post in the area attached to the front steps. I don't know if it would have collapsed or not-but called anyway. The ramp and the powerchair were a God-send.

ISSUE WITH THE VA

My issue with the VA began January 6, 2014. The VA doctor suggested my husband receive a home-based physician's assistant to come to our house, making it easier for him to receive care. The VA doctor said, "The service was not for everyone." He didn't express why. But I found out in full force being January 6th. **His statement was an understatement**.

My husband is a stroke victim and does not talk or walk. His mental ability is fine but he talks very few words. The VA PA began home-based medical service on 1-6-2014. She came too often and was grating -like fingernails on a blackboard. We fired her in March. Unknowing to us she still had her fingers in our business instead of returning us back to Tallahassee VA outpatient clinic.

On 5-22-2014 following VA protocol I canceled an appointment, on 5-23-2014, a Department of Children and Families worker came to our house. My husband was alone-he let her in the house because she was with a police officer. I had gone to Tallahassee to take our grandson to his mother's store. My husband wears an emergency button when I am away.

The VA PA reported me to the abuse hotline for **CANCELLING an APPOINTMENT** and withholding medical services and treatment and medicines to my husband **for years**.

EVENT WITH FLORIDA DCF WORKER

The DCF worker spoke to me on phone as I was checking out of my daughter's store, with my daughter nearby, I received a call on my cell, it was Perry Florida Police dispatcher in Perry. The dispatcher said, "Officer Bass wanted to talk to me." Assuming my husband had pushed his emergency response button, but Bass handed the phone to Florida DCF worker, they were both in my home but DCF worker refused to tell me why she was in my home and was evasive repeatedly stating she needed to talk to me because she couldn't understand my husband. **"Of course not "HE HAD A STROKE", he does not talk or walk.** Comprehension intact.

The DCF worker was evasive and not forthcoming with anything. I had my youngest daughter call my oldest daughter to run over see what was the matter as I did not know if husband had heart attack. DCF worker would tell me nothing beyond she needed to talk to me. My aunt and oldest Daughter went to my house. I headed to Perry.

First thing out of DCF's mouth to my daughter, **"I HAD CANCELED VA appointment.".** the other things which are beyond my control such as (1) **MAKING appointment** unless I feel husband needing immediate care, (2) **writing RX** , I call when needing refills. (3) **RX medical services**, which VA has provided bathing services through Doctors Memorial Hospital in Perry where we live, (4) **Ordering wheelchair lift and lighter powerchair** required for my car as my lift is damaged. VA PA was responsible for this and failed to do so.

To contradict allegations, my oldest Daughter showed DCF worker newly refilled medicines, bathing schedules signed by Doctor's Memorial Hospital worker on 5-22. All **things contradicting everything alleged by VA's PA,** she did it out of spite because we fired her. She did not see my husband shake his head in agreement to firing her, so her aggression was toward me.

When I rushed home with my youngest daughter, I began calling VA clinic's administrator in Tallahassee for protocol rules for canceling appointments. No changes.

When I did speak to DCF worker later in day, (after calling VA admin for protocol for canceling appts), she was still evasive and said she was returning to Perry next day (Saturday before Labor Day), I was on speaker phone with daughter to hear, I told DCF I did not want her to come to my home she could talk to me on phone. She was driving and it was late and she didn't want to talk then. We waited all day Sat. for DCF worker to call. She never did.

On Tuesday following Labor Day, I called DCF worker and she said, "I was the **perp** and etc. THEN, she said, "I, **DIDN'T WANT TO TALK TO HER BECAUSE SHE WAS BLACK."** I told her, "I don't know what color she is and I don't care if she was poke-a-dotted and told her "WHAT SHE SAID WAS RACIST." I cannot see her color through the phone, yet I hear from her voice that she was Black. DCF worker also said, "Officer Bass was fearful of me." That was strange because I have no guns and I am a short fat 68-year-old woman (at that time) and he has a gun.

I filed a complaint with the Perry Police department against VA PA for false allegation of abuse. Days later I called and police officer said case would be closed because they have nothing. To which I responded, "They have not taken the statements of my aunt and daughter."

I send my aunt down to make her statement and a police officer said "They had to wait until DCF finished their investigation and they would send them the report."

I also filed a complaint against DCF worker with DCF Inspector General's office. There is no way DCF worker could use UNBAISED evaluation of allegation. She later called and said she was "closing case as UNSUBSTANTIATED". ALLEGATION WAS CLEARLY FALSE ALLEGATION and against the law. I knew, my filing a complaint against DCF worker, that she would not file compliant of false report against VA PA.

I called DCF worker's supervisor to complain as to the classification, but she said she was the final person to close the case. I have not received a copy of the report. Not only has VA PA caused me and my family great duress and stress, along with embarrassment the DCF person acted in a racist and insulting manner. Apparently, making false reports do not apply to VA PA; had it been made by someone else they would have been arrested per Florida Statutes.

A few weeks later, I canceled an appointment with the VA because we do not have a new lift for my car and the VA hospital in Gainesville, Florida is too big for me to push my husband around in manual wheelchair. The very next day, I received a call asking why I canceled appointment. I asked the person was she prompted to call by VA PA. I HAVE NEVER HAD A CALL FOR CANCELLING AN APPOINTMENT with this doctor. Of course, she didn't acknowledge she was prompted by the VA PA. I assume she did it.

GETTING VA RECORDS

I demanded records of the VA PA visits. Some days a VA social arrived with the VA PA. The records show, the social worker wrote: "I was unkept and neglectful of myself". Although, **she did acknowledge that I was working on a rental property to get it ready to rent.** Her statement angered me. I bathe every night and I wear specific clothing (scrubs and shorts, along with work boots) when repairing and cleaning rental houses. Although, these clothes are clean they are stained with paint and other things used in the clean-up process. This statement by the social worker was uncalled for and demeaning to me.

VA CLINIC OPENED IN PERRY AND HOME-BOUND CARE

We started VA services with Perry VA Clinic. If you have a hard time getting spouse into VA building, they will sometimes come curbside. This happened once in Perry clinic.

We began getting home-health services from several organizations. My husband became bed-ridden the last year and the nurses and bathers were great in all organizations.

I became angrier when he became bedridden. I told him he proved me a liar, when I had to start wiping his butt.

A young Black man (Freddie) came to visit long after my husband's older White friends stopped visiting. He always called our daughters his sisters and my husband and I, his parents. My husband inherited him when he bought a gas station in a Black neighborhood. My husband took him (about twelve-years-old) under his wing. Taught him how to count money, pump gas and etc., when he came to visit the two of them would have a good laugh and Freddie would sing to him, sometimes he played the piano. When I was helping my husband with repetitive sentences, Freddie added, "My titties hurt." They always had a good laugh at that.

My husband could say my name clearly and he did often, repeatedly. When Freddie came, my husband would call my name repeatedly. When I came to his room, he would say, "Nothing".

And they both would laugh and laugh. My husband knew how much it annoyed me to be interrupted for nothing.

I screamed and hollered a lot, because I hate caregiving. I know God is going to punish me for it. But, my reward for being married to this man so long-was nothing. The time was never right for getting a divorce. But it was always way past necessary. I get angry when I hear young people get a new house when they first get engaged or married. He always teased at getting a new house for our family of five.

We have been carrying around a concrete "Venus" fountain to put at the head of our pool. (A fountain head he insisted upon buying to tease me with.) A pool he never intended to build or a house he never intended to buy or build. I am still mad at him for not buying the Spanish house which was offered on a silver platter. I always will be.

THINGS TO DO IMMEDIATEDLY AFTER A DIAGNOSIS

1) **Check to make sure your name is own your spouse's bank account.** My name was not and I did not know his salary income. My youngest daughter went to the credit union and got the president to add my name to his account so that I could pay bills.

2) **Get power of attorney.** When my husband came home, I got a power of attorney. The Clerk of Court would not take it. Although, I have paralegal training (I wrote it myself) they wanted another one. So, I took my husband to an attorney and had them write one. Then, I filed the document with the court.

3) **Change everything into your name.** Take the spouses name off all property, vehicles too. Make sure these changes are recorded with Clerk of Court.

4) **Write the spouses' will and get it notarized.** A will, then is nothing but a "directive" and does not have to go through probate because they own nothing. It gives a guideline for distribution of any material belongings. In other words, it tells exactly what the spouse wants to give each person.

5) **Locate insurance policies.** Upon the spouses demise, call all insurance companies for instructions to file. Usually they require a certified death certificate to make a claim.

6) **Get at least 10 certified death certificates.**

7) **An autopsy is not necessary if a person dies within 10 days of seeing their doctor. An autopsy is not necessary if the person is home-bound and has visiting nurses**. You call the home-bound services office **first, immediately after death**. No one else. The home-bound service nurse will rush to your house and conduct necessary procedures. The nurse writes the death certificate and gets it certified. She calls funeral home for pick-up. She also waits until pick-up before leaving home.

Although, these are not the only things needing done; these suggestions are a start.

My husband died April 2019, an hour after the nurse left our house.